Umbria

the Heart of Italy

Umbria
the Heart of Italy

HARALD KELLER

145 Photographs by Konrad Helbig

including 5 in color

A STUDIO BOOK

THE VIKING PRESS · NEW YORK

UMBRIEN LANDSCHAFT UND KUNST

COPYRIGHT © 1959 BY ANTON SCHROLL AND CO., VIENNA

UMBRIA THE HEART OF ITALY

TRANSLATED FROM THE GERMAN BY MICHAEL HERON

COPYRIGHT © 1961 BY THAMES AND HUDSON, LONDON

PUBLISHED IN 1961 BY THE VIKING PRESS, INC.

625 MADISON AVENUE, NEW YORK 22, N.Y.

LIBRARY OF CONGRESS CATALOG CARD NUMBER: 61-10423

TEXT PRINTED IN HOLLAND

ILLUSTRATIONS PRINTED IN AUSTRIA

CONTENTS

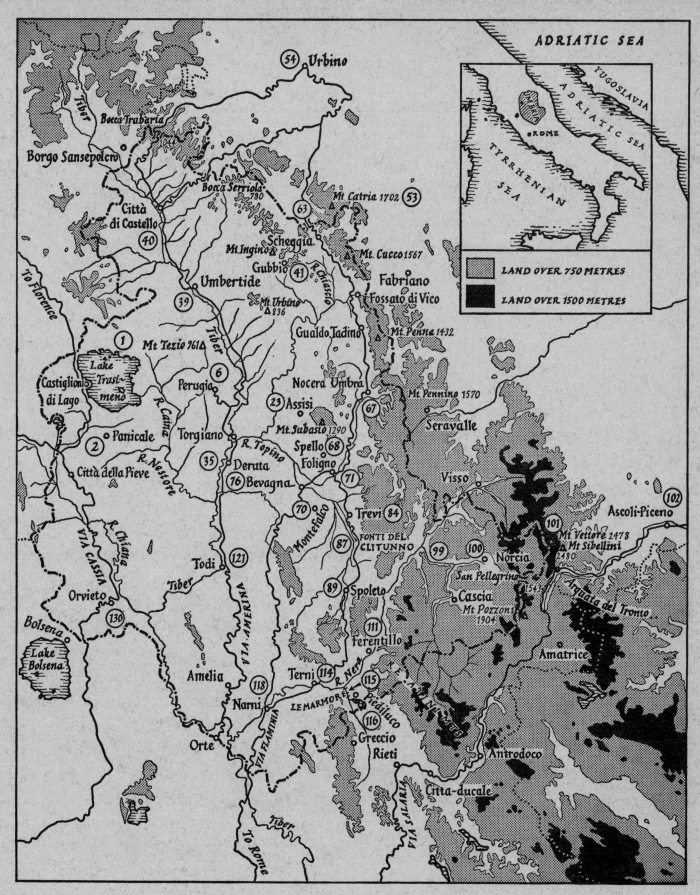

MAP OF UMBRIA: THE NUMBERS REFER TO THE PLATES

INTRODUCTION

EVEN on their first visit to Umbria most people will arrive with a rough idea of the region's general features — its towns, mountains and valleys — drawn generally from an acquaintance with the legend of St Francis. The whole district is steeped in associations with the saint's life-story — from Gubbio on the north-east border, where St Francis tamed the savage wolf, to the rocky cliff of Greccio in the south, which is already Sabine country and where in 1223 the saint first celebrated Christmas with a real crib and a live ox and ass. The closer we come to Assisi in the centre of Umbria, the town where St Francis was born, lived and died, the greater are the number of memorials to his piety. In the Pianura north of Bevagna he delivered his sermon to the birds; on the largest of the three islands in Lake Trasimeno where he stayed during Lent in 1223, visitors are still shown the marks on a massive rock left by the passionate penitent when he knelt in prayer. On one of the roads leading to the Tiber valley, he betrothed himself to Poverty who was passing by unrecognised in the company of two nuns. In Foligno he sold all his worldly possessions so that he could restore the little church of San Damiano out of the proceeds.

There are Franciscan monasteries, dating from the Order's foundation, scattered throughout the wild solitudes of the mountains surrounding the plain of Umbria. St Francis himself built seven cells on the broad wooded slopes of Monte Luco which tower above Spoleto — the nucleus which later grew into a monastery. Above Assisi, on the road to Subasio, lies the hermitage whither the saint sometimes retreated and which later became the home of the first Franciscan hermits. These Franciscan settlements can be found on the mountain slopes right up to the borders of Umbria, from Fontecolombo above Rieti to Le Celle in a wild gorge near Cortona. The radiant light which bathes mountain, hill and plain makes it easy for a stranger to understand how the saint came to be inspired to write the *Canticle of the Sun* in this particular landscape.

The art galleries and museums of Europe offer the visitor a second approach to Umbria, for in the paintings of Perugino and his close disciple the young Raphael, the very essence of the Umbrian landscape seems to have been captured for all time. Raphael's Madonnas with Christ and the young John, and the sacred events in Perugino's panels and frescoes are painted against a background of long rhythmic mountain ranges and smooth hill-tops bathed in a soft milky blue light. Slender, pliant trees with delicate, feathery foliage like giant meadow-grass waving in the wind lead the eye back into the depth of the picture. The faces of the saints are noble and serene; their gestures calm and gentle. There is a solemn reserve, a religious hush to be found in these panels which is quite foreign to Tuscan or Emilian pictures.

Should the visitor to Umbria have done any reading on the region, it will probably have been confined to Gabriele d'Annunzio's *Le Città del Silenzio*. The second book of the *Laudi*, called 'Elektra', written in 1904, contains poems about ancient towns in northern and central Italy, with a sonnet sequence on the towns of Umbria as its centre-piece. Using the language and images of Art Nouveau, d'Annunzio deliberately portrays these towns and villages as period pieces, peopling them with male and female dummies created only in order to wear historical dress. He describes priors descending the steps of the Palazzo Communale at Perugia, Benozzo Gozzoli painting at Montefalco, the Gattamelata, a ghostly shadow in bronze armour, passing through the Piazza at Narni. But he has no feeling at all for the appearance of the towns themselves and the way they fit into the landscape.

Of these three presentations of Umbria only the one based on the Franciscan legend still stands the test of time. And the image of Umbria it enshrines will be as valid and up-to-date in centuries to come as it was when the legend first came into being 700 years ago.

Nor do the painters give an accurate impression of Umbria. Perugino's is an idealised landscape which never varies and has as little in common with the real Umbria as the fabulous processions of kings, ambassadors and princesses in Pinturicchio's pictures have with everyday life in the narrow streets of Umbria's towns. The Umbrian landscape is infinitely richer and more varied, far more wild and melancholy, than one would ever imagine from the pictures of the Umbrian painters of the Early Renaissance. They had no eyes for its grandeur and romantic profusion; for the savagery with which the rivers have cut out their beds in the limestone massif over thousands of years; for the hopeless, abandoned quality of the treeless pasture-land, reminiscent of Tibet's grey-brown barren slopes and hills, near the borders of the Marches; for the bare Cubist shapes of Subasio or Monte Vettore.

8

But the picture of Umbria sketched by Gabriele d'Annunzio has vanished fastest of all. Art Nouveau has itself long since become a period piece. Within a few decades improved communications and industry have changed the face of a countryside which had remained unaltered for centuries. Even with the advent of railways in the second half of the 19th century, it was only possible to serve a limited area of a mountainous district like Umbria. In spite of one or two remarkable tunnels and viaducts (e.g. between Spoleto and Norcia) the railway system was tied, by and large, to the main roads in the valleys. Things only began to change with the coming of the car and, even more important, the bus. Even the most remote mountain villages, which are still without running water so that housewives have to fill their copper jugs at the well morning and evening, now have daily services to the next village, to Perugia and even to Rome. A small out-of-the way town like Amelia, for example, has seven services daily to Montecchio, Porchiano, Orte, Terni, Narni, Orvieto and Rome. Everywhere it is the same. And the cinema, wireless and television have also played their part in broadening Umbria's outlook.

Still more important is the fact that the Old 'Umbria verde' which Carducci praised in his famous verses, has been split in two by industrialisation. North Umbria has remained green farming country, but in the south-west hydraulic power from the Northern Apennines of Umbria and the Marches, which has mostly had to be artificially diverted to the Terni basin, has created a highly developed industrial area with humming turbines and smoking furnaces. In addition to the iron-foundries and armament factories established in the second half of the 19th century, there is now the electrochemical industry, which produces ammonia and calcium-carbide. Terni, which had only 57,000 inhabitants in 1950, had almost reached the hundred thousand mark eight years later, and as the town suffered serious damage from air-raids during the last war, it has undergone a double transformation. New street layouts have taken the place of former building sites and the reconstruction of public buildings has created new squares. Immediately below Narni is a new dam, which is a centre for the generation of electricity. When the Italian government announced in parliament in the early spring of 1958 that they were going to close down the lignite mines at Spoleto within two years, there was considerable alarm in the town, for out of a population of some 14,000 individuals, 1300 families earn their living by mining. The rapid industrialisation of southern Umbria has had to be taken into account administratively. When the kingdom of Italy was divided up into provinces in 1860, the

9

whole of Umbria was included in a single province. In 1927 Terni, in the south-west, as an exclusively industrial district, was made into a separate province in order to cater for the entirely different needs of its population. Consequently Umbria has developed, during the last few decades, into a district with conflicting interests in the economic and cultural spheres.

Shepherds and their flocks still roam through the northern half of the territory, Umbria Verde proper, especially the eastern border district, following a tradi-tional way of life governed by the seasons, like their ancestors before them. This year-round nomadic life, known as the *transumanza*, affects both eastern and western Umbria. The flocks which have wintered in Latium and the Sabine district are brought from the west and driven up to the Monti Sibillini at the beginning of June, while on the opposite side of the region the shepherds drive westwards from the Adriatic coast to Subasio, above Assisi. When the spring grass in the Campagna around Rome has been cropped and the pasture in Latium burnt up by the heat, the flocks begin a vast migration. They are driven slowly towards Umbria and then across it, climbing from sea-level to a height of 5,400-6,000 feet where they can expect cooler temperatures and richer pasture. Four months later, at the beginning of October, the flocks return to their pens to winter. But obviously the large-scale systematic settlement of the Tuscan and Latin Maremma has adversely affected the *transumanza*. Winter quarters have become fewer and the size of the flocks has already begun to decrease.

Apart from Piedmont and Lombardy, Umbria is the only district in Italy which has no coastline. It fits snugly into the west side of the curve of the Apen-nines where they bulge out towards the Adriatic, so that the highest mountain ridge forms its eastern boundary. Present-day Umbria is shaped roughly like a rhombus whose northern tip lies to the west of Borgo San Sepolcro on the Bocca Trabária pass leading to Urbino. The southern extremity is marked by the road junction where the Via Flaminia leaves the Tiber valley to curve off to the north-east, following the valley of the Nera; this happens at a point approximately level with Viterbo, not far from Città Castellana, the last coaching station, where Goethe spent the night before his arrival in Rome in 1786. That is to say, the southern tip of Umbria lies virtually on the outskirts of the Holy City. Monte Vettore (8,033 ft), one of the Monti Sibillini group, forms the eastern tip of the rhombus and Umbria's western border stretches beyond Orvieto almost to the shore of Lake Bolsena. Umbria is one of the smallest cultural divisions in Italy, for the whole rhombus is only about 84 miles long and 66 miles wide. Southern

Tuscany and northern Latium block the way to the Tyrrhenian sea and the region is separated from the Adriatic by the Marches.

It is evident that present-day Umbria does not represent a natural land division surrounded by natural borders, but the last bulwark to which the hard-pressed original inhabitants managed to hold on after a series of heavy defeats and losses of land. The Umbrians did not retreat into their mountain valleys voluntarily. Pliny and Cato considered them to be the original inhabitants of Italy, the earliest rulers of Etruria (now Tuscany and north Latium) from which the Etruscans drove them out, and also of the Adriatic coast between Rimini and Ancona, which they lost to the Gallic Senones. In the north, too, the Umbrians originally spread far across the Apennines to the south bank of the Po. But by historical times they had long been driven back from the coast and become inhabitants of an inland mountain district. Strong-points in use as early as the prehistoric era became the region's permanent borders, which have not altered essentially since Augustus divided the Italian peninsula into provinces. It was inevitable that Umbria should play a secondary role in Italian affairs. Her main waterway is the Tiber; it runs through the whole province from north to south, but on its estuary lies Rome, effectively cutting Umbria off from the sea. The drainage system alone is clear evidence that the country was open to the south-west from very early times and that the natural tendencies for development were towards the Latin shore. Given the numerical, cultural and military superiority of the Etruscans, expansion northwards was, of course, out of the question. And so, hemmed in on all sides, Umbria became a cramped region of woods and mountains, with a surface area of which six per cent is flat, forty-one per cent hilly and fifty-three per cent mountainous. She had no such advantages as the vast stretches of pasture land of the Maremma, or the large, brilliant urban populations of the Tuscan hill towns.

The Umbrian mountain ranges run parallel to the Northern Apennines from north to south. They are characterised by flattened ridges and broad bulges rather than sharp peaks and precipitous slopes — a phenomenon caused by the action of water during the Tertiary period.

This system of gentle undulations and flattened hilltops rings the southern side of Lake Trasimeno at a height of about 1,900 feet, rising to 2,100–2,400 feet around Perugia and Gubbio and reaching 3,900–4,220 feet towards the eastern edge of the Pianura Umbra (Subasio, above Assisi, is 4,212 feet high) without any change in its over-all shape. Hills with rounded tops give way to enormous ridges with broad humped tops, but the contours remain the same. The massive sandy and clayey rocks which are found here cause the peculiarly dull greenish grey, rather monotonous, colours of the barren hills and humps. On Umbria's eastern border, in the central and southern section of the Umbrian Apennines south of the Scheggia pass, enormous limestone peaks which seem quite alien to the flat-tened plateau-like character of the Umbrian mountains appear more and more frequently, although they do little to alter the over-all effect of the landscape. Nor do they provide land for grazing any longer. South of the valley of the Nera these limestone peaks become part of the highlands of the Abruzzi. So that really these naked crags with their light silver tones rising above ever-green *macchia* are only typical of the eastern tip of the region, the mountains which form the border facing the Marches beyond the Norcia basin.

However, Umbria's mountain formations are less important than the valleys embedded between these mountains; it is in them that the real life of the province goes on. They follow the mountain ridges and run in a south-south-easterly direction. The rivers provide connecting valleys between the main basins, which means that they form the province's principal lines of communication. The basins were originally lakes and as a result fertile alluvial soil has been deposited on their floors. Some of these have dried up only within recorded historical times, as in the case of the biggest of these basins, now known as the 'Pianura Umbra', which stretches for 34 miles from the slopes of Perugia south-eastwards to between Assisi and Bettona; this was the 'lacus umber', and only lost its water in the early Middle Ages during the reign of King Theodoric; there were, in fact, extensive bogs in the section of the basin between Trevi and Foligno as late as 1563. Today Lake Trasimeno remains to give us a very good idea of how the basins of Gubbio, Gualdo, Tadino, Terni, Norcia and Cascia originally looked. The last of the Umbrian lakes, its sole source of supply is a watershed. The only reason that it is drying up more slowly than the others is that it has no outlet.

The towns are always situated on the slopes above, never on the floors of the basins which are only occupied by single farmsteads and rich *poderi* whose roofs peep out from amongst mulberry and hornbeam trees; the Gobelin tint of olive trees is not such a familiar sight here as it is in Tuscany.

The rivers whose valleys link up the basins have had to carve their way through numerous obstructions. The Tiber, which cuts very slightly into the floor of the valley near Deruta, is an exception. Usually the rivers and streams have to eat their way through the soil in narrow valleys with precipitous slopes and laboriously carve out a bed in the limestone massif. Narrow rocky passes formed by the relentless

12

force of water are so common in Umbria that a wealth of different names have been coined to describe them - *incisa* (incision), *gola* (channel), *forra* (gorge), *serravalle* (closure of a valley), *stretto* and *stretta* (narrow defile); the passes were, of course, key positions, both in time of peace and in time of war, and any visitor who spends the day walking or motoring through Umbria is bound to come across many of them: the steep valley of the Tescino near Strettura between Spoleto and Terni, the *gola* immediately behind Gubbio on the ascent to the Scheggia pass, the other *gola* in the Nera valley near Ferentillo, Serravalle in the Sordo valley between Norcia and Triponzo . . .

A country of woods, mountains and pasture-land welded on to the chain of the Northern Apennines, in many parts actually straddling the mountains, deprived of its former coastlines to east and west by its more powerful enemies, Umbria really seems to have been intended by history to become a remote agricultural district, self-contained and cut off from the turmoil of the outside world. If it escaped this fate, it was because of its special position in the centre of Italy with vital lines of communication running through it. For in it are situated low and easily negotiable passes through which the Marches, the Adriatic coast and the eastern plain of the Po could be reached without travellers having to climb above 800 feet. The more Rome tended to become the most important centre in Italy and the capital of an empire, the more Umbria was criss-crossed by extensive road systems and their offshoots. The Via Flaminia has to cleave its way to the Adriatic coast by crossing the Northern Apennines in a narrow gorge (the *gola* of Furlò). In the same way, the Via Salaria crosses the southern boundary of Umbria, and its route through the Tronto valley equals the defile at Forlò for wild romantic beauty. It reaches the sea near San Benedetto del Tronto.

The placing of the towns in relation to these roads immediately gives the clue to their age. Orte and Todi lie on the Via Amerina; Narni, Terni, Spoleto, Trevi, and Foligno lie on the new stretch of the Via Flaminia which was built in the early imperial epoch. Beyond where the classical and early mediaeval stretches join up again north of Foligno, come Nocera and Gualdo Tadino. The ancient town of Bevagna lies on the abandoned part of the Via Flaminia, while Spello and Assisi, the home of Propertius, are situated on minor classical roads on the other side of the Pianura. With the exception of Perugia, which could only form the terminus of Roman roads, Orvieto high up on its rocky perch between the Via Cassia and the Via Amerina, and Città di Castello, all the towns in Umbria lie on roads built in classical times. It follows that these three towns which are not included in the network of Roman roads must be even older than the others, and it is a fact that Perugia and Orvieto are Etruscan towns (Orvieto actually appears to have been unoccupied in Roman times), while Città di Castello (Tifernum) is an old centre of the Umbrian race with no Roman memorials or inscriptions.

All these Umbrian towns are perched up in the mountains. Perugia, Orvieto Panicale and Città della Pieve, even Orte (although administratively it no longer forms part of Umbria) are built on plateaux on high mountain massifs; Amelia and Narni occupy the summits of steep cone-shaped mountains; Spoleto and Trevi, Spello and Assisi, Todi and Gubbio are typical examples of towns built on the sides of hills. Often they sprawl vertically up the whole side (Trevi), sometimes they spread horizontally across them in terraces, in which case the street system consists of a series of parallel transverse alleys linking the terraces (Assisi, Gubbio). The mountainous situation of the Umbrian towns is a natural consequence of the dampness of the alluvial land forming the beds of the main basins. As a result, there is scarcely another province in the whole of Italy whose towns are so uniform as those of Umbria.

The visitor passing through them finds himself continually climbing steps and going down alleyways, and their distinctive architectural style is merely a result of local designers' attempts to build structures adapted to the sloping, multi-level sites. The architecture of Gubbio, for instance, is distinguished from that of other towns by the particular way in which its buildings are placed on the steep side of Monte Ingino. The lowest level of the valley floor is occupied by the 13th-century San Giovanni Battista; above it are the Palazzo dei Consoli and the Palazzo Pretorio, two tall 14th-century buildings, built on massive substructures and facing each other on the same terrace with an early 19th-century classical palace between them; next comes the Early Renaissance ducal palace of Federico da Montefeltre, who was born here; a step higher up is the cathedral, and crowning it all the mediaeval town wall. Each building differs from the rest in style and proportions, yet the total effect is one of harmony and no single building overpowers its neighbours. They all go to make up one unified whole. The same could be said of nearly all the Umbrian towns. At Assisi the temple of Minerva lies higher up the slope than San Francesco, which in turn is higher than San Damiano. It seems appropriate that the famous annual feast of the *Ceri* at Gubbio should centre round a foot-race in which heavy statues of the saints are carried up a very steep hill. And on the hill-top above each of these Umbrian towns is a *Rocca;* these are castles, which the stern Spanish Cardinal Albornoz had built during the Church's vassaldom to Avignon to keep the communes within the Papal State (they may be seen at Spoleto, Assisi, Todi, Narni, Piediluco and Orvieto).

In many respects the men who live in these towns and villages, and the scattered farmhouses of the Pianura, do not differ greatly from the inhabitants of neighbouring provinces. Like the farmers in the Contado of Siena, they take a great pride in their ploughing teams of regal white oxen, which look as if they were part of a procession to some ancient sacrificial altar until they are yoked to their vermilion carts. The Umbrians go off hunting on weekdays on their motor-bicycles, with shotguns slung over their shoulders and full cartridge belts strapped round their waists, with as much gusto as the rest of the Italians. If the Lake Trasimeno fishermen are asked what they do in the winter, they answer 'nothing' with the same bitter melancholy as all other southerners whose work is seasonal.

And the poverty in the mountain villages is scarcely any greater than in Latium, although it is unusual to see there, as we did in one of the highest villages in Umbria (4,722 feet), the inn crammed with local farmers, only one of whom had enough money to buy a glass of wine.

Yet Umbria has a flavour all its own. When Umbrians play *boccia* or cards together, when they make their purchases at one of the big cattle markets on annual feast days or haggle with the travelling pedlars who lay out their wares on the pavements, the atmosphere is more subdued than in, for example, Tuscany. They do not take the same conscious delight in acting a part when making a deal or arguing in a tavern; their gestures are more controlled and less extravagant.

Umbrians tend to have fuller cheeks and lips than other Italians, but the big black eyes like sloes which are supposed to be characteristic of them are not so common as is often supposed. They occur more frequently in Perugino's rare portraits and the many extant travel books than in reality. When Umbrians grow older their faces become round and smooth, quite unlike the eagle- and hawk-like profiles which are common in Tuscany.

Where the Tuscan is sceptical, the Umbrian is religious. Umbria is not only the country of St Francis and Iacopone da Todi, it is also the seat of the most concentrated popular devotion in Italy. It not only possesses the memorial church built over the home of St Benedict (Norcia), the church in which St Francis is buried, and the church in memory of the miracle of Bolsena (Orvieto Cathedral) — its hills and mountains are also dotted with pilgrimage churches and little chapels whose walls and altars are covered with votive gifts, from the Madonna della Neve high above the basin of Norcia to the Madonna delle Grazie above

15

Bevagna, from the Santuario della Madonna di Mongiovino half-way between Città della Pieve and Perugia to the Santuario of St Rita of Cascia, who was not canonised until 1900 but now draws the biggest crowd of pilgrims in the whole of Italy.

The private devotional sculpture, a prerequisite of which is an inner relationship between the image worshipped and the individual worshipper, was cultivated in Umbria to an extent unknown in any other Italian region. The Umbrians, with their great sensitivity and lyrical feeling, were strongly attracted by the German *Vesperbild*, which the Italians called *Pietà*. The German itinerant masters came down from northern Italy and received so many commissions that they frequently settled. But only in Umbria and the neighbouring Marches are late mediaeval *Pietà* groups found in such numbers that they give a comprehensive picture of the way in which the work of the German wood-carvers was adopted, imitated and given local characteristics by Umbrian carvers. Afterwards the theme of the Madonna with her dead son in her lap was taken up as a subject for painting. The commonest subjects in Umbrian rural *ex voto* paintings, most of which are found in the Nera valley, are, apart from the *Pietà*, the Madonna and Child, the *imago pietatis*, the scourging of our Lord and Saints Christopher and Sebastian. The *Pietà* was not the only motif popular with local wood-carvers. Beginning with the Madonna by Presbyter Martinus, dating from 1199 as we know from its inscription (Berlin, Museum), an unending stream of Madonnas Enthroned, Calvaries and groups showing the Descent from the Cross was produced in Umbria, which only the neighbouring territory round Siena can outdo in variety and richness of technique. It is clear from this profusion of wood carvings that St Francis's mystical fervour was handed down as a common legacy to the Umbrians and that it lasted throughout the Middle Ages.

In order to understand Umbria's history, and in particular its cultural development, one must appreciate that its political boundaries and its limits as an artistic entity are by no means one and the same thing. In fact, on all of its borders there have been complicated instances of overlapping and adjustment arising from the changing course of history. Città de Castello, for example, situated in the northern tip of Umbria on the main road in the Tiber valley, lies in a purely Umbrian setting, but its streets and squares look like those of a Tuscan country town. The artistic influence of nearby Florence predominates here, although from 1500 onward it formed part of the Papal State, thus sharing the political destiny of the other towns in Umbria. Its palaces were built by

16

Antonio da Sangallo the younger and Vasari and consequently there is a hint of Florentine austerity about its streets and public buildings which is quite alien to the average Umbrian town.

In Orvieto the reverse is the case. The landscape there has nothing Umbrian about it at all. The town, like so many of the old *villes perchées* of southern Etruria and northern Latium, is built on the flat top of a bare crag of dark honey-coloured tufa. Pitigliano and Sorano, Città Castellana and Nepi all grow out of massive formations of porous tufa. But there can be no doubt about the Umbrian character of Orvieto's art — it is the richest and most purely Umbrian artistic centre in the region, next to Perugia.

Administrative boundaries are always arbitary to a certain extent; it is more surprising that the natural geographic boundaries did not act as artistic barriers. Strangely enough, in spite of the towering ridge of the Apennines and the marked physical difference between Umbria and the Marches, fundamentally they form a single cultural entity. It is not as paradoxical as it seems to call Raphael, who was born in Urbino, the 'great Umbrian'. There are hundreds of ties between the artistic life of Umbria and the Marches despite the mountain range dividing them. The other great Umbrian painter, Piero della Francesca, who spent the greater part of his life in his native town of Borgo San Sepolcro on the border of Umbria facing Tuscany, often paid year-long visits to the academy at Urbino and appears to have been the outstanding artistic figure among the crowds of mathematicians and theoreticians of perspective who gathered round Federico da Montefeltre. The Duke himself built a palace in Gubbio a decade after he had begun his first palace in Urbino. The striking similarity in their design shows that the same artists were at work on either side of the mountains. The way they approached the problem of articulating a church façade was the same in both Umbria and the Marches. The hall, a type of interior very rarely encountered in the rest of Italy, was widely taken up in Umbria and immediately copied in the Marches.

The first culture of which we have any real knowledge is the Villanovan. These people, who may have sailed across the Tyrrhenian Sea to Tuscany from the other side of the Adriatic, laid the foundation of the civilization of the Etruscans. The distribution of their settlements was mainly coastal The associations with the sea in Etruscan art can be seen particularly clearly it the towns of the Maremma. At the time of their conquest of Umbria, the Etruscans shrank from the task of colonising the Northern Apennines and contented themselves with the coastal region. Perugia is the most easterly of the Etruscan confederation of twelve towns; there is no place in central Italy which gives a better idea of Etruscan architecture than Perugia, where the Arco d'Agosto and the Porta Marzia with their impressive walled towers represent the last word in Etruscan defensive building. The rich burial grounds below the town (the tomb of the Volumnii, the tomb of San Manno) complete the picture. Etruscan cemeteries with burial chambers have also been excavated at various points on the big hill of tufa on which Orvieto is situated.

One glance at the Roman buildings is enough to show that the new masters regarded the conquered territory primarily as a military transit area. The amphitheatres and ruined temples, sarcophagi and mosaic pavements in most Umbrian towns are not very impressive, unlike the bridges which carry the Via Flaminia over the rivers — the bridge over the Nera below Narni which Corot painted when more of it was still standing, the Ponte Sanguinario at Spoleto and the Ponte di Solestà over the Trento at Ascoli. On the other hand, Umbria has a unique collection of late classical buildings. In Rome and Milan only a few Early Christian churches of the 4th and 5th centuries have been preserved, and they have been repeatedly modified in later centuries. But San Salvatore outside Spoleto, the church in the Temple of Clitumnus near Trevi and the round church of Sant'Angelo at Perugia are perfect examples of Early Christian architecture and have come down to us almost unspoiled.

Unfortunately, little survives from the long centuries of the early and late Middle Ages. After the Lombard conquest, Spoleto became the capital of the dukedom in 569, but the traces of life left behind by the Lombards during the time of the migration of the peoples and the early Middle Ages are disappointingly few. And Umbria obviously remained provincial during Carolingian, Ottonian and Romanesque times. Only Sant'Eufemia at Spoleto reflects the new outlook of the great architects of western Europe. Charming as the two Romanesque churches in Bevagna are, Umbria possesses no examples of the elaborate ambulatories with their rings of chapels, which appeared in Tuscany, for example, in the 12th century, the projecting transepts whose cubes stand in harmonious relationship to the nave, the towers over the crossing, and façades with sculptures and magnificent marble encrustation which are found elsewhere.

Umbrian art attained its zenith in the 13th century. It is as if St Francis had provided the inspiration for artistic expression throughout the province. It was during his lifetime that the new universal style of French Gothic penetrated into

18

Italy. St Francis strove to put into practice the austere ideals of primitive Christianity and it is paradoxical that over his grave should have been built a church which for richness of architecture and decorative painting càn only be compared with Chartres Cathedral. But the church is now cited as an example of European architecture of the time. The shape of the interior and the system of supports were adopted from Anjou, and the church was decorated by the most famous painters from every province in Italy – the greatest of the Umbrians, Romans, Florentines and Sienese. This collaboration by artists from different provinces was to be repeated 200 years later in the Sistine Chapel in the Vatican. Shortly before 1300, in Dante's early period, the marble cathedral of Orvieto was built; its façade is unique in western Gothic for the audacity of its conception. It was at this period that the stately administrative buildings of the communes rose in Perugia, Gubbio, Orvieto and Todi, each one nobler and more impressive than the last. Nor could the hall church have gained such a footing in Umbria or led to such wonderful results as in San Fortunato at Todi had not active contact with the Gothic architecture of countries beyond the Alps still been maintained around 1300. Even the interiors of churches of the mendicant orders, which elsewhere conformed to type, acquired a certain individuality in Umbria during this period.

It is not surprising that Umbria's artistic energies flagged after rising to such heights and that by and large the 14th century was unfruitful, unlike the two centuries flanking it on either side.

Although individual Renaissance buildings in Umbria, such as the Ducal palace at Urbino and the Madonna della Consolazione outside Todi, enjoy world renown, the Umbrian art of this period is largely dominated by painting and painters: Piero della Francesca, Perugino, Pinturicchio and Raphael. With the death of Perugino (1532) the flame of Umbrian painting was more or less extinguished, for the lavish output of the Baroque period – there is scarcely another province in Italy with so many 'baroquified' churches as Umbria – was widespread but did not penetrate beneath the surface. The grandiose art of Federico Barocci is no longer to be viewed in purely Umbrian terms.

Architecture provides the easiest clue to an understanding of what is peculiarly Umbrian in Umbrian art. The favourite Umbrian interior is the hall, which is quite unknown in other parts of Italy (apart from a few scattered Romanesque buildings in Lombardy). In contrast to the Christian basilica, the hall church does not draw the gaze in any single direction. In the basilica the architectonic forms are such that the eye is drawn irresistibiy on towards the high altar in the choir; in the centrally planned building the spatial composition is centred on the point directly below the top of the dome. But in the hall church with its aisles of equal height and width, the composition is allowed to develop towards the sides without limitation. Whereas everything is related to the axes in the basilica, in the hall the eye can wander freely in every direction and delightful diagonal vistas are revealed. However much it gives an impression of height inside, every hall church stands squarely on the ground and its exterior gives a solid horizontal accent to a town's appearance. Consequently, the design was primarily adopted by those western cultural areas whose inhabitants had an inherently balanced and thoughtful, or even stolid character: Poitou, Westphalia, Swabia and Austria. And so, when their art was at its peak, the Umbrians too opted for a style of interior which avoided harsh contrasts of line, allowed spatial boundaries to remain vague, and aimed and soft, delicate modelling and shading. The sequence of Umbrian hall churches began as early as the 13th century with San Andrea at Orvieto, San Fortunato at Todi and San Domenico at Perugia, and entered on a second golden age in the 15th century with Perugia Cathedral, the Casa Santa at Loreto and the cathedral at Ascoli Piceno. Nearly all the churches in Ascoli today are hall churches.

The centrally planned building, like the hall church, avoids the extreme emphasis of the basilica. Neither of them exhibits the tendency to exaggerated height which is so often apparent in the nave of the basilica. The three, or even five, aisles of the hall church seem to be trying to merge into one another sideways, just as the space at the crossing in a Renaissance church of central plan establishes a pleasing relationship with the surrounding and supporting galleries, exedrae and chapels. These Renaissance churches were deliberately designed with harmonious proportions related to the scale of the average human figure and this may have endeared this architectural style to the Umbrians even more than the hall church. The only district whose passion for centrally planned churches can compare with Umbria's, is Lombardy. But even there an Umbrian, Bramante, was responsible for making the style popular. There is hardly a single Umbrian altar picture of the Early Renaissance which does not use the idealised architecture ot an airy central church as a background to the main subject, from the panels of 1473 showing the legend of St Bernardino (Perugia, Pinacoteca) and Perugino's fresco of St Peter receiving the keys in the Sistine Chapel to Raphael's Sposalizio (Milan, Brera). It was in the 'seventies too that a number of churches of this type began to be built, culminating in the Madonna della Consolazione below Todi, which is today definitely considered to be the classic example of a High Renaissance centrally planned church. But even during the two Baroque centuries a wealth of such churches was still being built in Umbria. The surprising continuity in Umbrian taste can be seen from the way in which church façades were treated throughout the centuries. The Umbrians consistently strove to preserve the uniformity of the façade, to eschew wide, gaping, recessed portals which broke up the surface and to avoid clustered pilasters and columns. Reliefs were kept extremely flat and, on the more magnificent buildings, were replaced whenever possible by mosaics which did not project out from the wall surface at all. The almost universal type of articulation was by division into flat panels, inside which the virgin surface was interfered with as little as possible. The late Romanesque façade of San Pietro outside Spoleto with its wealth of relief work (about 1200) provides an example of this manner of composition at its best. The same style appears again in the façade of Orvieto Cathedral, built in 1310, this time using some of the features of French cathedral Gothic. Orvieto was the only Gothic cathedral in the west with the lower storey of its façade completely covered with reliefs. The division into panels is not necessarily effected by mouldings in relief; in numerous Umbrian churches it is achieved by encrustation, by the alternate use of white and raspberry-coloured marble. The Marches also took over from Umbria this manner of articulating façades. The sixty-four rectangular panels into which the front of SS. Vicenzo e Anastasio at Ascoli Piceno is divided are in direct descent from such buildings as Assisi Cathedral. As regards sculpture, the Umbrians were never really at home with stone carving. They preferred wood, which was easier to work with. It seems as if there was something in the Umbrian artistic temperament which shrank from the laborious struggle between chisel and obdurate marble. In any case, apart from the façade of Orvieto Cathedral, created by a Sienese who had become completely assimilated to the Umbrian milieu, there is no important memorial of Umbrian sculpture left. The Perugian-born sculptor Vincenzo Danti (1530-76) had no chance to express himself in his native land and artistically speaking belongs entirely to the circle of Florentine mannerists. His contemporary, Ippolito Scalza of Orvieto, was only of local importance. Umbrian painting was astonishingly late in developing. True, the frescoes in the nave of the lower church of San Francesco at Assisi — the earliest ever painted in the region — bear witness that there was a most important school of Umbrian painting using very unusual colours as early as 1270. But it must have died out soon afterwards, for Umbrian painters took no further part in the decoration of the great Umbrian saint's memorial church. The Romans Cavallini and Torriti, Cimabue and Giotto from Florence, the Sienese Simone Martini and Pietro Lorenzetti, had the field to themselves. Nor were there any Umbrian centres of painting of more than local importance during the latter part of the 14th century; in Perugia the commissions were given to Meo da Siena who had settled there, to Taddeo di Bartolo, Luca di Tomé and Domenico di Bartolo - all of them Sienese.

A genuinely Umbrian use of colour first emerges in the 15th century at a time when the best opportunity must have already seemed to be past. The painting generally thought of as 'the Umbrian School' and displayed under that name in museums and galleries was created during the lifetime of only two generations of artists, beginning with *The Legend of St Bernardino* in 1473 and ending with the death of Perugino in 1523. The Florentines painting in Umbria during the first three-quarters of the 15th century still set the tone to such an extent that the indigenous Umbrian feeling for colour could not break through. It was only when the delight in the clean, light, ringing colours of Benozzo Gozzoli and Filippo Lippi had disappeared that the mild and subdued tonality of the Umbrian altars and frescoes was gradually able to develop. By 1466 Niccolo Alunno's palette already contains the dark wine-red and thick inky blue which, together with a dark mossy green, were to form the basic colour scheme of all Umbrian panel pictures. Benedetto Bonfigli, who painted from 1445 onwards, was the first to use warm crimson lake instead of the Florentine red, which is always tinged with cold violet, and to adopt a cream yellow which merges into light brown, thus avoiding the shrill saffron yellow tones. The only noticeable disruption in the steady development of an Umbrian colour scheme occured when young Umbrian painters studied in Florence. Fiorenzo di Lorenzo, for example, belongs completely to Verrocchio's circle. Perugino, on the other hand, remained faithful to the typically Umbrian use of colour, although he eagerly accepted the new techniques he learned in Verrocchio's workshop for goldsmiths and sculptors. In the *Adoration of the Magi* (Perugia, Pinacoteca) the subject is set against a subdued landscape; there are no nostalgic blue distances, no glittering water reflecting the changing silhouettes of the banks, no sailing clouds. He clothes his figures in brown, not gold, brocade. There is no trace of Verrocchio's lemon yellow; a slate-coloured blue and dull brick-red have taken the place of the hard bright Florentine blues and reds.

Was this type of colour, only in use for two centuries, truly Umbrian? Or was it not merely peculiar to Perugino and his circle? These are questions which

22

might reasonable be asked, if it were not for the existence of the frescoes of *c.* 1270 in the nave of the lower church at Assisi which reveal a delight in the same subdued colours in the same sort of arrangement, and the dozens of Umbrian church façades whose encrustations in red and white checkerboard patterns testify to a similar taste in colour.

The narrative tone of the pictures of the Umbrian School is as mild and gentle as the colouring. There is a wealth of incident but none of it is unpleasant or violent. Anyone who has stood in front of the panels of the *Legend of St Bernardino* or Perugino's frescoes in the Collegio del Cambio at Perugia, or wandered through Pinturicchio's cathedral library at Siena, or seen the decoration of the Borgias' chambers in the Vatican, has to admit that they show a very idealized aspect of life. Umbrian painting has no contact with reality and that explains why it presents very few examples of portrait painting (apart, significantly enough, from one or two portraits of children and youths). If any art has ever served to create an ideal dream world in which the spectator is required to forget the stern realities of the battle for existence, then it was Umbrian painting at the beginning of the 15th century.

Living conditions at that time were less bearable in Perugia, Spello, Foligno and Nocera than in the rest of Italy. A permanent state of war existed; town gates had to be kept closed because marauding bands of soldiers roamed through the countryside and burnt the crops; while inside the towns the partisans of the various noble factions killed each other with dagger and poison. Justice had long since been thrown overboard. If a victor laid hands on his enemy, he became a savage. During the conspiracy against the Baglioni, the rulers of Perugia, Astorre Baglione was murdered in his sleep 'and thereupon the traitor Filippo plunged his hand into the dead man's breast and forcibly tore out his heart, and bit it... and with that he dragged him down the staircase like a peasant and common man and laid him in the street as naked as the day he was born.' The following year, after the siege of Acquasarta, a castle in the territory of Todi, an extortioner fleeing from the nobles of that town was laid low. 'And then everyone ran past to procure a bit of his flesh and they ate it raw, just like dogs and swine, so that nothing remained of his poor miserable body, and even if he had been a giant he would not have provided enough meat for his enemies.' Thus the Chronicle of Perugia for the years 1492-1503, which appears under the signature of Francesco Matarazzo. To judge from their work, Umbrian painters were blissfully ignorant of, or indifferent to, the real life of the streets and squares in the towns of the period. Their art is simple and uncomplicated; in this respect the Umbrians are like the Swabians: they can only see those elements which contribute to a harmonious and pleasing picture of life — a peaceful, lyrical world where time stands still, an innocent fairyland.

But the Umbrian painters who were driven by a daemonic urge to use their energies on a grander scale quickly outgrew their Umbrian surroundings. Great artists could not develop in Umbria and the Marches. Perugino and Raphael had to go through the cleansing fire of Florentine art to find themselves; Bramante went to the court of Ludovico il Moro in Lombardy; Galeazzo Alessi became a great master-builder in Late Renaissance Genoa, when he gave the city the face it still retains; Federico Barocci first found himself after studying Correggio's work at Parma, and Rome had the same effect on the mature Raphael.

A walled garden closed to the outside world — that is the picture presented by Umbrian art just before the beginning of the High Renaissance. But when Bramante, building St Peter's in Rome for Pope Julius II, chose a central plan, and when Raphael painted the *School of Athens* in the Vatican Stanze, it was evident that the legacy of their native Umbria had survived through all that they had experienced in the Eternal City with its classical atmosphere. The problems they now had to solve were already familiar to them. The Roman works of these two geniuses mark both the highest achievements of Umbrian art and its absorption into the main stream of a universal classicism.

1 LAKE TRASIMENO   View of the northern shore near Passignano from Castiglione del Lago.
The fourth biggest of the Italian lakes. Fed by a water-shed which lies between the Arno and the Tiber, Lake Trasimeno is the last of the Umbrian lakes and it, too, is gradually drying up. Originally the basins of Gubbio, Norcia, Terni, etc., were all filled by similar lakes. Lake Trasimeno is never more than 22 feet deep. Because it is so shallow, there is a delightful play of light and colour on its surface, far surpassing that of the better-known lakes of northern Italy. The turquoise and opalescent tones are especially beautiful. The Isola Maggiore is the only one of the lake's three islands which is still inhabited. In 1328 it was settled by a colony of Franciscan monks who were hosts to St Bernardino of Siena and Pope Pius III (1459) during the 5th century. Today the western shore is occupied by a fishing village consisting of a single unpaved street built like a courtyard. There are only four farms on the Isola Polvese and a game-keeper's cottage on the neighbouring Isola Minore.
    The famous battle in which Hannibal and the Carthaginians annihilated the Roman army under Consul Caius Flaminius was fought near Passignano in the late June of 217 BC.

2 PANICALE looking towards Lake Trasimeno.
Although this mountain village, perched on a ridge near the southern shore, was the birthplace of Masolino, the Early Renaissance painter, he chose to live and work in Florence and had no connection with Umbrian painting. The town has managed to preserve its ancient character and appearance right up to the present day. In the top left-hand corner is the Isola Polvese on Lake Trasimeno.

3 LAKE TRASIMENO   The south-eastern shore with the Isola Polvese from the summit of Montemelino. This photograph gives a particularly good idea of the way the lake is drying out. Whereas reeds densely grow along only parts of the other shores, the southern shore is completely lined with small islands of sedge. The spaces between these are filled with mud which is still too soft to farm; further inland, fields are under cultivation.

4 This out-of-doors tinsmith's workshop illustrates the simplicity of rural Umbria. Only the south-west has been industrialised.

5 Everyday life in PANICALE continues in surroundings unspoiled by modernisation.

6 PERUGIA View of the Porta della Mandorla from the upper town. Like other towns in Umbria and Tuscany, Perugia has preserved the original Etruscan wall round its old town centre. It is built entirely of travertine blocks and has an overall length of nearly 2 miles. Because of the shelving terrain round the city, which stands on a plateau, the wall follows a highly irregular course. The Porta della Mandorla is the town's south-western gate. In the 13th century it was converted into a Gothic gate of the same width but lower. We know this because the Gothic pointed arch sits appreciably below the Etruscan round arch, whose haunches can still be made out. The two stone imposts jutting out into the opening are also Gothic. When first built it would obviously have had a mediaeval defense gallery on top instead of its present-day top storey. Judging from its narrowness, the steep road which leads up to the gate seems typically Gothic, but in fact it could scarcely have been any wider in Etruscan times.

7 PERUGIA Fontana Maggiore and Palazzo dei Priori. Throughout the Middle Ages, the most vital problem for a mountain town was ensuring an adequate water supply. Whereas Siena did not succeed in installing the magnificent fountain in its main square, after a good deal of trial and error, until the 15th century, Perugia arrived at a solution which is equally admirable from all points of view – technical, hydraulic and artistic – as early as the 13th century. In 1254 it was decided to build the conduit and water was finally brought to the town after more than 20 years of preparatory work. It then became necessary to build a fountain, which was completed in 1278. An inscription in Gothic capitals round its basin gives the names of the men who commisioned it and those who constructed it, and tells us that Niccolo Pisano and his son Giovanni collaborated on the sculptures and reliefs. The fountain stands in the middle of the Piazza between the southern façade of the cathedral and the Palazzo dei Priori. To compensate for the slope of the ground, the lower basin is set on a tiered base. Above the two stone basins there is a bronze bowl in which stands a group of three caryatid-like female figures. The water shoots out above their heads. The upper basin stands in the lower one and is supported by 58 columns, of which only the 24 outside ones are visible. The composition of the fountain owes its wonderful rhythmic vitality to the fact that the lower basin has 25 sides while the upper basin has only 23, so that they never coincide but are always slightly staggered. Only the lower basin is decorated with reliefs; the corresponding spaces on the upper basin are left empty and there are statuettes at the corners instead.

8, 9 PERUGIA Reliefs, symbolizing May and November, from the above. The reliefs on the lower basin introduce several unconnected themes; the seven liberal arts, the foundation of Rome, animal fables, etc., as well as a complete sequence showing the months of the year, with two reliefs devoted to each month. Both show people engaged in some type of activity normally associated with the month; the left-hand panel also contains the appropriate sign of the Zodiac. Similar pictures of the months form part of the decorations of the façade of every 13th-century Gothic

26

cathedral. The panel for May shows a nobleman and his wife going hawking, the wife with a falcon on her wrist. Facing the knight, the sign of Gemini. In the November panel a team of oxen plough the fields and the seed is sown. Above the ploughman, the sign of Sagittarius. The free, spontaneous movements in which both man and beast are caught here imply that this was Giovanni's work – only the clumsy design of the panel with the team ploughing seems likely to have been by his father, Niccolo. When Giovanni Pisano undertook this work in Perugia, he had just returned from France, where he would have seen pictures of men in action in the relief friezes on Rheims Cathedral. The empty background is obviously derived from Byzantine ivory work.

10 PERUGIA   Part of the south façade of the cathedral. White marble facing in lattice-work design; the light red marble ground can be clearly seen through the quatrefoils. The panels probably date from the 13th or early 14th century. According to local historians of the Baroque period they were made for Arezzo Cathedral but were brought to Perugia as loot after a victory over the Aretines in 1375. The Aretines are supposed to have won back a number of panels in 1371 when the fortunes of war changed. It is unlikely that the quatrefoils were originally decorated with figures as the old authors state – unless they were thinking of incised line drawings or intaglia, like those on the floor of Siena Cathedral. The marble facing has been in its present position since the construction of the cathedral (begun in 1437), whose south side was so nearly completed in 1445 or 1449 that it was able to house the trophies of war.

11 PERUGIA   Main doorway of the Palazzo dei Priori facing the Corso Vanucci. As soon as an additional site had been bought, a second block was added to the oldest part of the late 13th-century palace, whose main façade looks on to the Piazza. It was built between 1333 and 1353. The main doorway, which is richly decorated and recessed, ends in a semi-circular archivolt instead of a pointed arch, although it dates from the height of the Gothic period. This is less surprising in Italy than it would be in northern Europe – in many parts of the country the local dislike of the northern pointed arch led to the Romanesque round arch being preserved until it became fashionable again in the Early Renaissance. The designer of this doorway, who is thought to have been a follower of Giovanni Pisano, took as his models the three round-arched doorways of the west façade of Siena Cathedral (begun in 1284) and the central door of Orvieto Cathedral (begun in 1310). Giovanni Pisano had already used lions to support the columns flanking the portal of the cathedral at San Quirino d'Orcia (near Siena). It is obvious from the stick-like, rigid statuettes on the tympanum that this doorway dates from at least one generation after Giovanni Pisano's death. The three marble figures represent the local saints: Bishop Ercolano the Martyr, St Lawrence, to whom the cathedral is dedicated, and St Louis of Toulouse who was one of the main witnesses to the early Franciscan movement. The griffins on the corbels above the columns are the heraldic emblems of Perugia.

12 PERUGIA   Collegio del Cambio: *Apollo* by Perugino. In 1452 work was begun on a house for the guild of Perugian money-changers. The frescoes in the main hall were painted by Pietro Perugino between 1499 and 1507. The vaulted ceiling is decorated with paintings representing Apollo and his chariot (in the square central panel) and allegories of the planets (in the surrounding panels); these must date from about 1500, shortly after the decoration was undertaken. Grotesques of the type which adorn the gable panel became extremely popular and were eagerly imitated after the discovery of similar classical decorations on Nero's Golden House, excavated near the Colosseum in Rome towards the end of the 15th century.

13 PERUGIA, PINACOTECA   *St Bernardino of Siena restoring to life a girl who had fallen into a well*, 1473. By the Master of the Legend of St Bernardino. The picture in this photograph, together with seven others, decorated the panels of a cupboard originally in the Oratorio di San Bernardino; this cupboard was used to house the flag or *gonfalone* of the brotherhood of the same name. One of the pictures bears the inscription '1473 finis'. The panels are variously ascribed to Perugino, Pinturicchio and an anonymous artist. The very fact that this cycle is attributed, however tentatively, to the leading masters of Early Renaissance painting in Umbria means that it is probably one of the earliest products of a truly indigenous school of Umbrian painting. This panel in particular shows quite clearly who was the main inspiration of the new young school. In its treatment of light rather than of objects, this picture shows the unmistakable influence of that great painter of light and air, Piero della Francesca, who was the first to portray the space between figures in action as filled with air rather than 'empty'. Although every fold of the pearl-grey Franciscan cloak is clearly drawn, more important is the modelling of figures and clothing by the light-drenched atmosphere. In the architectural background behind the main figures of the legend of St Bernardino, we catch our first glimpse of the extravagant use of painted architecture which was later to dominate Pinturicchio's frescoes in Siena and Rome.

14 PERUGIA   Arco d'Agosto from the Palazzo Gallenga Stuart. The most northerly gate of the original Etruscan fortress, built towards the very end of the Etruscan domination, about 100 BC, or possibly even in the time of Sulla. The lower three-quarters of the structure are completely uniform, that is, the gate and the two flanking towers (the right-hand lower is hidden by the Baroque palace in this photograph) were built as a whole. The change in the size and arrangement of the stones about half way up the tower does not indicate that the two halves were built at different times. The Etruscan part of the town gate proper ends with the series of stocky Ionic pilasters with shields between them. The large arch in the upper storey (now bricked in) belongs to the Roman period. Perugia was actually conquered by Octavian in 40 BC, but the inscription *Augusta Perusia* on the keystone of the great arch cannot have been engraved before 27 BC when the Emperor first adopted this honorific title. The Roman additions also date from this time. A second smaller

inscription, *Colona Vibia*, on the frieze immediately below the pilasters is in memory of Emperor C. Vibius Trebonianus Gallus (251–53 AD), who came from a distinguished Perugian family.

The addition of an Early Renaissance loggia about 1500, and of other features during the Baroque period, to the left (and eastern) half of the gate has added a not of charming irregularity to the strict symmetry of the original composition.

Right, the Palazzo Gallenga Stuart, a magnificent Baroque building (1748–58) by P. Carattoli, which now houses the Italian University for Foreign Students, well-known for its summer schools (founded in 1926).

15 PERUGIA looking north from the Porta Sole. Perugia's town-plan, like Siena's, is curiously spider-like. In both towns the Piazza represents the body, from which the legs radiate in all directions. Narrow ridges and spurs run down from the plateau on all sides. They are only wide enough to contain a single street or so which has to conform to the contours of the ground. Between these 'suburbs' cultivated fields run right up to the town centre. Naturally these streets were not enclosed by the town walls in Etruscan times. They were only gradually walled in during the Middle Ages, after 1321. As in Siena, churches, especially those of the mediaeval monastic communities, were situated at the far ends of such suburbs. In the 13th century the Arco d'Agosto was still the only gate to the north, but in 1326 another northern gate was built beyond the Early Christian round church of Sant' Angelo, thus bringing the suburb within the town fortifications. The walls in the centre of the picture, built by Ambrogio Maitani, brother of the architect of Orvieto Cathedral, are from the same period.

16, 17 PERUGIA Oratorio di San Bernardino: façade. Reliefs by Augustino di Duccio.
16 Left-hand side of the doorway. Angels making music.
17 Tympanum. St Bernardino of Siena transported to heaven between angelic musicians.

In 1461, ten years after St Bernardino's canonization, an oratory for the brother-hood founded in his name was built on the spot where he best loved to preach. As there were no outstanding Umbrian sculptors in the 15th century, the commission was given to the Florentine master Angelo di Duccio, who had just distinguished himself in the decoration of the Tempio Malatestino at Rimini (1447–55). A disciple of Luca della Robbia's, Duccio worked on the façade of the oratory at Perugia from 1457 to 1461. The sensitive Umbrians probably most valued his skill in portraying strong emotion. But the Etruscan influence which emerges in his sharp linear treatment of drapery is equally appropriate to such an ancient Etruscan town as Perugia.

18 PERUGIA Sant' Angelo: interior. This 5th-century round church consists of a central space whose once-brightly-lit clerestory is supported by a ring of sixteen columns. Surrounding this is a lower outside wall from which four separate chapels (no longer extant) led off, three of square plan and one a horseshoe-shaped apse. The columns

29

of the outer wall are of different heights and materials (shafts of granite, cipollino and black marble) and were looted from another, earlier, building. Like the majority of Early Christian round churches of the 5th century, the building was not vaulted but had a wooden roof (compare Santo Stefano Rotondo in Rome, Kal'at at Simân in Syria and probably also the so-called 'baptistery' at Canosa in Apulia, whose ground plan is remarkably similar to that of Sant' Angelo). In the 14th century eight Gothic arches were added to the central space to support the mediaeval roof. Work has been going on since 1950 to restore the church to its original Early Christian condition.

19 PERUGIA San Pietro: view of the nave. The church, which is one of town's oldest, was redecorated in the Late Renaissance, from 1556 onward, and extravagantly painted. The only remnants of the original mediaeval columned basilica are the arcades of the nave, supported by eighteen Ionic columns made of grey marble and oriental granite taken from the Temple of Venus. The interior is quite unique among Perugia's churches in that it makes a markedly Venetian impression. This is enhanced by the enormous canvases of Antonio Vassilacchi, called Aliense, a pupil of Tintoretto, which line the upper wall of the nave. They were painted between 1592 and 1594 and depict ten scenes from the Old and New Testaments. An eleventh picture on the inner entrance wall shows the genealogy of the Benedictine order.

20 Etruscan cippus. (Museo Etrusco Romano, PERUGIA)
Stone chests of this kind (tapering off in a cone shape) were used to hold the ashes of those who had been cremated. The vessel has a mouth at the top through which the ashes were poured. The sides were usually decorated with strips of bas-relief. The detail shown here covers almost the whole of the front of an Etruscan cippus from the last quarter of the 6th century. It portrays women dancing at the graveside.

21, 22 The tomb of the Volumnii near PERUGIA Situated 3 miles from the Porta San Costanzo on the southern slopes below the town, facing the Tiber valley, near the Perugia-Foligno road. Discovered in 1840 during the building of a road to Assisi.
        A rectangular building (11 ft 10 ins × 24 ft) shaped like a classical house has been excavated in the grey-brown tufa. A steep roof, a stone copy of a wooden roof, rises above the walls at an angle of 45 degrees. A tablinum is joined on to one end of the hut, while burial chambers are ranged along the sides. Although the tomb was apparently never forced there are no signs of burial-treasure; and obviously there were few actual burials here, because only the tablinum contains sarcophagi (the side chambers are empty). The family of the founder ceased using the tomb in Roman times. For five generations the members of a family who bore the surname of Volumnius, extremely common throughout Italy, were laid to rest here. It must have been a very distinguished Etruscan family, for these are, without doubt, noble tombs. Neither the inscriptions nor the other contents of the burial chamber give any clues as to date. But the burial chamber must have been built around 70 BC

and the last burial took place about 10 BC, a whole generation after Augustus's punishment of Perugia and the loss of Etruscan independence. So the sarcophagus of the last Volumnius can no longer be classified as an example of Etruscan art; dependence on Rome shows clearly in its design and decoration. This sarcophagus of Publius Volumnius dates from the *Ara Pacis* (13–9 BC) and should be appraised with those dates in mind. The most splendid and still purely Etruscan memorial is that of Arnth Volumnius (died about 65 BC), who had the tomb erected for his grandfather, father, himself and his descendents. His double coffin stands on a high pedestal on the front of which is a painting of the door to the underworld. On the capital of the column on each side of the door sits a female messenger of death or Vanth (plate 21).

These winged creatures are wearing short upper garments tied with crossed ribbons of the type worn by the Greek Furies. The Vanth has a funeral torch in her left hand and is holding up the ends of her long cloak with her right hand. Art historians have long sought to prove the Etruscan influence on Michelangelo's style by comparing these messengers of death from the tomb of the Volumnii with the great Florentine's statues.

In the museum over the mausoleum are exhibited a large number of Etruscan burial urns, which were found in the 38 burial chambers of a necropolis which also contains the tomb of the Volumnii. Most of these urns are made of travertine and bear traces of colour. The architectonic type predominates; only a few of them have a recumbent statuette of the dead person on the lid.

1 Lake Trasimeno

2   Panicale, looking towards Lake Trasimeno

3   The south-eastern shore of Lake Trasimeno with the Isola Polvese

4 Tinsmiths working in the open

5 Market-day in Panicale

6 Perugia. View from the upper town

7 Perugia. Fontana Maggiore and Palazzo dei Priori

8—9 Perugia. Fountain, with reliefs symbolizing May and November

10   Perugia. Part of the south façade of the Cathedral

11 Perugia. Main doorway of the Palazzo dei Priori

12 Perugia. Collegio del Cambio: Apollo, painted by Perugino

13   Master of the Legend of St Bernadin: A Miracle of St Bernadin

14 Perugia. Arco d'Augusto

15 Perugia. Looking north from the Porta Sole

16 Perugia. Oratorio di San Bernadino: reliefs on façade

17 Perugia. Oratorio di San Bernadino: relief on tympanum

18   Perugia. Sant'Angelo

19 Perugia. San Pietro

20 Etruscan cippus

21   Detail of the Tomb of the Volumni near Perugia

22 Detail of the Tomb of the Volumni near Perugia

23 View of San Francesco and the Pianura Umbra from the citadel of ASSISI This shows how the saint's memorial church, like all the churches of the mendicant orders in Italy, was built on the edge of the town, in this case outside the town wall towards the west on one of the last spurs of the castle hill jutting out towards the Pianura. Perugia is visible on the mountain which cuts off the Pianura in the top right-hand corner of the picture.

24 The Tescio valley, with ASSISI in the background, in springtime. The castle (in the centre of the picture) dominates the town.

25 ASSISI San Francesco from the south.
The massive substructures, which were necessary here because of the steeply sloping ground, were built to last for ever.
The monastery was begun in 1230 by the General of the order, Fra Elia da Cortona, and planned on a grand scale from the outset because it was also intended to serve, when necessary, as the Pope's residence. The substructures of the south façade were begun in 1367, but the southern wing of the monastery was only half finished in the 14th century. Building was resumed and the monastery extended westwards in 1420, and it was completed in 1443.

26 ASSISI San Francesco: apse.
The five-sided choir of the upper church develops almost imperceptibly out of the semi-circular apse of the lower church. The transition is marked only by a fine knife-edge moulding. Barely fifteen years earlier the architect of the choir of Bamberg Cathedral had, in typically Late Romanesque fashion, treated the same architectural problem of basing a polygon on a cylinder by introducing much horizontal articulation between the two forms, thus making the transition more gradual. At Assisi the solution is purely Gothic. The lines of the building are all vertical, the façade uniformly plain (see the façade of Orvieto Cathedral). In addition, the Umbrian architect obviously decided against letting the choir jut out bluntly beyond the walls of the transept. So he placed two round towers at the angles between choir and transept; these tone down the sudden protrusion of the choir, conceal the right-angled corners and provide a gradual and gentle transition to the transept walls.
On Pope Sixtus IV's orders the choir was surrounded with a two-storeyed cloister (it has only one storey on its east side) whose roof forms an open platform at the level of the windowsills of the apse of the lower church.

27 ASSISI San Francesco: the Piazza Inferiore, church and campanile. St Francis died in 1226 and was canonised in 1228. Pope Gregory laid the foundation stone for his memorial church on the day after his canonisation. Building proceeded astonishingly fast and the whole structure was finished more quickly then almost any other in the Middle Ages. The saint's remains were transported to the lower church and buried under the high altar in May 1230, so that it must have been sufficiently advanced by that time to receive them. It was completed in 1239 when Fra Elia was deposed as General of the Order. The upper church was begun in 1245 and finished in 1253, when it was consecrated by Pope Innocent IV. The upper and lower churches were conceived as a single unit. Fra Elia may or may not have been responsible for the master plan; whether or no, he was certainly the driving force behind its execution. Both churches have a single nave, consisting of four roughly-square bays, with a projecting transept. The turret-like buttresses placed at the junctures between the bays to take the pressure of the arches on the outer wall are derived from southern French models. The architects of Mediterranean France disliked the open stress system of flying buttresses and piers developed in northern France around 1200, and substituted for this system a more solid, heavy arrangement of supports to take the thrust (Albi Cathedral, Niort, Bordeaux, St Leurin). The flying-buttresses which supplement the cylindrical buttresses at Assisi today were only added for additional strength after the earthquake of 1279. The interior of the upper church is French-inspired but the campanile and the façade with its Late Romanesque rose window and plain triangular gable are faithful to the local tradition. The Piazza Inferiore is surrounded by an Early Renaissance cloister. The steep double flight of steps leading from the square to the façade of the upper church was given a new balustrade in 1743.

Adjoining the façade on the left is the benediction loggia of 1607. The high open porch in front of the entrance to the lower church is an Early Renaissance construction of 1487.

28 ASSISI The lower church of San Francesco: *St Francis and two angels* (detail from a fresco by Cimabue in the northern transept).

Although it was intended from the very beginning that the interior of San Francesco should be decorated with religious frescoes, there was a delay after the main structure was completed. The decoration of the lower church was not taken in hand until 1270, and the paintings in the upper church were not begun until the last decade of the 13th century. The choir and transept of the upper church were painted in accordance with a master plan by the Florentine Cimabue. In the lower church there is only one fresco by him; this is situated in the northern transept next to the crossing and depicts a Madonna enthroned with angels. The strict symmetry of the composition is thrown out of balance by the introduction of St Francis on the right-hand side. With palms raised the saint exhibits his stigmata; the wounds in his side are visible through a hole in his cloak. St Francis had only been dead for about 70 years when the picture was painted. But this is no guarantee that it shows an actual likeness of the saint, because no authenticated portrait of him has survived. Even in literary sources it is impossible to find a detailed description of St Francis's face. He began to be portrayed in two completely different ways almost immediately after his death: the Italians showed him as young and beardless, while the Byzantine portrait-type represents the saint (who died aged 44) with a pointed beard and as a man prematurely aged by his sufferings. Cimabue used the Byzantine type and painted an emaciated monk's face with hollow cheeks, bristly beard and deep-set eyes like glowing coals. Even the angels who stand beside the Madonna's throne are Byzantine angels.

29 The Upper Church, ASSISI Fifth fresco from the Legend of St Francis: *The saint renounces his father*. Designed by Giotto.

Twenty-eight frescoes representing the life of St Francis run round three sides of the nave of the upper church, filling the lower part of the space reserved for decoration, immediately above the visitor's head. In this fresco the saint is renouncing his father. He has just handed back his worldly clothing and the infuriated old man has to be forcibly restrained by friends and relatives from attacking his son. The Bishop of Assisi covers Francis's nakedness with his cloak, thus symbolically receiving him into the bosom of the Church.

Giotto's authorship of this series of frescoes has long been the subject of academic controversy. The striking discrepancy between the brilliant composition of many of these pictures and the coarse, careless execution of some of them can be most readily understood if we assume that Giotto was primarily the master designer who made large outline drawings on the prepared surface but left the actual execution to his pupils, while he carried out commissions elsewhere. At all events the cycle must have been painted before Giotto went to Padua, which places it between 1295 and 1305.

30 ASSISI The façade of Santa Chiara in the spring.

St Clare (1194–1253) was St Francis's first female disciple and founder of the Poor Clares, a Franciscan order of nuns. The church was begun in 1257 and the saint's remains were buried here in 1260. It was consecrated by Pope Clement IV in 1265.

In plan and elevation the building follows San Francesco very closely: a church with a single nave divided into four bays, a projecting transept and a choir forming five sides of a decagon. However there is no second church. Because the painting of the interior came to a halt after the completion of the frescoes in the transept, the lofty unarticulated walls of the nave still seem to be waiting for their decoration and produce a rather austere effect. The encrustation of the façade is carried out in alternate red and white stripes. The campanile at the side of the apse, unlike the tower of San Francesco, still has its conical spire.

31 ASSISI Cathedral of San Rufino: the right-hand side doorway.

32 ASSISI   Cathedral of San Rufino.
This cathedral, dedicated to the 3rd-century bishop and martyr, went through many metamorphoses before attaining its present-day appearance. According to an inscription it was begun in 1140.

The building took a long time; there is evidence that it was still in progress in 1210. In 1217 the unfinished sections threatened to collapse. It was consecrated by Pope Honorius III in 1228.

The façade is an example of the rather simple plain surface which is so typically Umbrian. It consists of two distinct sections. The two storeys below the gable date from about 1200, which was also the period when the façade of San Pietro at Spoleto (see plates 98 and 100) was divided up into rather similar panels. The gable with its pointed arch, above the three Late Romanesque pierced rose windows, can scarcely have been built before the end of the 13th century.

The great central rose window is surrounded by the symbols of the four evangelists and is supported by three female figures like mediaeval caryatids. Four carved animal figures project from the gallery.

The campanile dates from the 12th and 13th centuries. The right-hand side doorway, like the other two doors, is richly decorated with carvings. At the base of the door jambs crouch two griffins, a motif adopted from Lombardy. In the centre of the lintel is the Lamb of God, at the top of the archivolt the cross of Christ, while the other medallions contain a mixture of fabulous and real animals, and rosettes. On the tympanum, two birds (peacocks?) drink out of a vase – a late mediaeval copy of an Early Christian motif (Ravenna).

The interior behind the façade is now pure Late Renaissance as the result of work done in 1571.

33 ASSISI   The temple of Minerva.
Goethe, who walked up from the valley on 26th October 1786 and averted his gaze as he passed by 'the monstrous substructures of the churches piled Babel-wise one over another', (in one of which St Francis lies buried), was delighted by the façade of the temple above. 'And behold, before my eyes stood the noble edifice, the first complete memorial of antiquity I had ever seen. A modest temple, as was fitting for so small a town, and yet so perfect, so beautifully conceived that it would stand out anywhere... I could not get my fill of looking at the façade and seeing to what brilliant effect the artist had done his work here... cannot express the transformation which took place within my mind as I looked at this work...'

The temple dates from the Augustan period. The cella behind the façade was extended in 1539 and converted into the Christian church of Santa Maria sopra Minerva, which was decorated in Baroque style in 1634.

34 ASSISI   View from the castle hill.
The first mention of a castle above Assisi dates from the time of Frederick Barbarossa, when in 1174 the German Chancellor, Archbishop Christian of Mainz, had

conquered Assisi and entrusted the town to Konrad of Islingen, who styled himself 'Duke of Spoleto and Count of Assisi'. He must have built the *rocca* or at least refortified an existing building, because at the time it was counted among the strongest places in Umbria (next to the castles of Gualdo Tedino and Cesi). After the death of Emperor Henry IV the citizens of Assisi razed it to the ground in 1198. It lay in ruins until a formal treaty was signed in 1367 between the town and Cardinal Albornoz, who had been commissioned by the curia at Avignon to regain the papal territory in central Italy. Not only was the *rocca* rebuilt but the *rochetta* was added at the eastern edge of the town facing Subasio, which was obviously a weak spot in the town's defences. The *rocca*, high up on the hill, consists of a trapezoid girdle of outer walls with square towers at the corners. Inside is the castle proper with its towering rectangular keep. The towers added by the Renaissance Popes Pius II and Paul III are not visible in this picture.

35 The Tiber valley near Deruta.
The Tiber's bed is flat; the river makes only a shallow impression in the valley bottom as it winds its way through the remains of the ancient forests of alders and poplars. This determines the character of the landscape from Perugia to Todi.

36 The characteristic Umbrian features with their full lips and dark eyes are typified by this young peasant.

37 Pietro Perugino' *Portrait of a Youth* has the large sloe eyes which are traditionally ascribed to Umbrians, but are less frequently found in real life than in art and travel literature.

38 DERUTA   Pilgrimage church of Madonna di Bagno: column with votive tablets.
Deruta is famous for making ceramics, an art first mentioned in 1387, but the town is certainly older than that date. Ceramic-making reached its zenith in the first half of the 16th century. As a result, the pilgrimage church of Madonna di Bagno, which is a half-hour walk to the south of the town, is completely covered with hundreds of majolica votive tablets, which were mostly dedicated in the late 17th and 18th centuries. The sole rights to supply votive tablets for this place of pilgrimage were vested in the local majolica industry for almost three and a half centuries. The fact that votive gifts of other materials were never hung there was solely due to the advocacy of the priests in charge of the pilgrimages who probably recommended this uniform style of decoration on commercial rather than aesthetic ground. It would be difficult to name another place of pilgrimage in which the grouping of votive gifts was made to conform to such a uniform stylistic tradition.

39 CIVITA RANIERI near Umbertide.   Castle.
A typical mediaeval structure which was added to in the Renaissance.

40 CITTA DI CASTELLO Piazza with the Palazzo del Governo. The dome and campanile of the cathedral are visible in the background. The piazza, like the rest of the town, has a decidedly Tuscan appearance, which is not remarkable in a town situated in the extreme northern tip of Umbria where all the communications are dependent on Tuscany. Thus the Baroque façade of the mediaeval Palazzo del Governo maintains a severe Tuscan reserve, exemplified by the thin strip of pilasters dividing off the topmost portion of the building and the virtual absence of Baroque surface articulation. The other façades of the palace giving on to the longer sides of the square are similar in appearance. During the Renaissance Antonio da San Gallo the Younger and Vasari supervised the building of the palace.

41 The Vale of GUBBIO from the west. The extremely fertile alluvial country of the dried-out basin is surrounded by hills of sandstone and marl which are gradually being eroded by weathering. Gubbio can be seen in the middle of the picture, at the eastern edge of the plain which lies in front of a deep cutting in the hills; this cutting leads to the Scheggia Pass. Top right: the lofty limestone chain of the High Apennines with Monte Catria.

42 View down on to GUBBIO from the campanile of San Francesco. The town lies on the slope of Monte Ingino. In its present form it is a unified piece of 14th-century town planning. Only the long building on the floor of the valley in the foreground was added later, in the 15th century. It is one of the oldest factories in Italy, the spinning mill of the wool workers' guild (Tiratorio dell'arte della Lana). Immediately above the roof of the factory can be seen the façade of the 13th-century church of San Giovanni Battista. All the smaller buildings are overshadowed by the Palazzo dei Consoli, dating from the early 13th century, on the left, and the Palazzo Pretorio of 1349, on the right, which enclose the Piazza della Signoria with their mighty substructures. The early-19th-century Palazzo Ranghiasci-Brancaleoni with its three groups of classical columns and pilasters is a fitting termination to the far side of the square. Above its flat roof can be seen the palace of the Dukes of Urbino, built by Federico da Montefeltre, while the side and campanile of the cathedral appear above the Palazzo Pretorio. Just above the campanile is a part of the 14th-century town wall.

43 GUBBIO Palazzo dei Consoli and Palazzo Pretorio.
The decision to build both palaces was taken by the *comune* on 19th January 1322. The architect was the native master Matteo di Gianello Maffei, called Gattapone, who later practised widely in Umbria as Cardinal Albornoz's architect. Although the *gonfaloniere* and the consuls were able to start using their official quarters in the Palazzo dei Consoli in 1346, the Palazzo Pretorio, begun in 1349, was left unfinished. It was originally intended to serve judicial purposes and provide offices for the *Podesta*, the *Capitano del Popolo* and the other legal officers. There is a 16th-century extension on the east side.

The flat composition used in Umbrian church façades, without reliefs or breaking up of the surface, is equally typical of mediaeval lay buildings in Umbria, and we have a classical example of it here. (The only sections with reliefs, the portal and the two flanking bifora on the first storey, are actually the work of another artist, Angelo da Orvieto, from 1332 to 1337, and seem out of place here.) The monumental gravity of the Palazzo peters out with its built-on wing facing the valley; this terminates in a charming third-storey loggia.

44 GUBBIO   The arched substructures of the Piazza della Signoria. Built as the foundations of the two palaces and the Piazza in the first third of the 14th century. The substructures are 58 feet high and about 48 feet deep. They are divided into six main sections, but the subdividing of these was never completed. The two sections facing the Palazzo Pretorio show that a floor halfway up was intended to divide the gigantic vaults into two storeys, the lower of which would also have been vaulted. They were used, as the need arose, as a slaugher-house, armoury or store-house for oil and corn. If the building had been completed, the smaller spaces would have been used as prison cells.

45 GUBBIO   Alley with 'doors of the dead'. The houses in the western, older part of Gubbio exhibit a strange architectural feature which is much rarer in other towns in Umbria (such as Assisi or Nocera): the 'doors of the dead'. (In this picture one is shown immediately above the old woman's head.) They are very tall, narrow door-ways to dwelling-houses; their thresholds are generally about 3 feet above street level. The popular explanation of these narrow doors is that they were special entrances kept permanently closed except after a death, when they were opened to allow the coffin to leave the house. This explanation is most unlikely. The tendency today is to regard these 'doors of the dead' as the sole entrances to mediaeval houses. While shops, craftsmen's workplaces and store-rooms had doors at ground level, private houses had high thresholds and narrow entrances to the upper stories so that they could be defended more efficiently. If no danger threatened, a small wooden ladder was used to reach the door from street-level; this could easily be removed if the house had to be put in a state of siege.

46 The feast of the Ceri in GUBBIO   Every year on 15th May the town celebrates its great feast; its inhabitants' behaviour during this has led to their being known as 'I matti di Gubbio' (the madmen of Gubbio). Traditionally, all Gubbians who are away from the city try to return home for the Ceri festival which takes place on the eve of St Ubaldo's day. The ceri themselves consist of two massive wooden octahe-drons, one on top of the other, with a combined height of 18 to 21 feet. There are three of them belonging to different trades, each of which was originally identified with a certain section (contrada) of the town. The masons' cero is topped by a wooden statuette of St Ubaldo, the town's patron saint, the shopkeepers' (in this picture) by one of St George, and the farmers' by one of St Anthony Abbot. For the rest of the

year the *ceri* are kept in the church of St Ubaldo on Monte Ingino high above the town; they are brought down on the first Sunday in May. Shortly before noon on 15th May, in the Piazza della Signoria, there is a contest in which each of the teams compete in mounting their saint on their *cero* and raising the whole into the air in the shortest possible time. This is followed by the *Mostra*, when teams of young men from each *contrada* run through the streets carrying their *cero* in procession. Each team has its own distinctive, brightly-coloured costumes; these are, of course, no longer the original mediaeval ones. The *ceri* are so heavy that the teams have to be changed during the running, which naturally involves considerable skill and practice. At noon officials, guests and participants sit down to a great banquet in the main hall of the Palazzo dei Consoli. About 6 o'clock in the evening the *ceri* are brought down to the town from the cathedral and blessed by the bishop, who is also present when the statues are first brought out at noon. They are then carried to the starting point in the Piazza della Signoria, where the mayor gives the signal for the start of a race from the balcony of the Palazzo Pretorio. Amid the pealing of an alarm bell and the indescribable yells of the crowd, the *ceri* are now carried up the hill to San Ubaldo.

While the race goes through the narrow streets, the spectators watch anxiously as the statuettes sway backwards and forwards from one side of the street to the other. The runners cover in 13 or 14 minutes the precipitous track to San Ubaldo which in the normal way it takes at least 40 minutes to walk. The path is so narrow that the three teams dare not overtake each other. Consequently the race is more like a mediaeval procession than a modern athletic race. At night the dismantled statues are carried down to the town again in a torchlight procession. The origin of the feast remains obscure. One theory sees the *ceri* as the annual victory feast for some decisive battle during the town's mediaeval history. None of the countless local feasts of other Italian towns (the Pallio of Siena, Giostro del Saracino at Arezzo, Gioco del Ponte at Pisa, etc.) have quite such a savage and passionate character as the *ceri*. When the runners, who have physically given of their utmost, are relieved of their burdens and sink down exhausted by the side of the road, it is only too easy to believe in the antique origins of the feast and see these modern races as descendants of some Dionysian cult.

47 GUBBIO Interior of the cathedral. The cathedral, a hall church, was under construction from 1240–43; the façade dates from the beginning of the 14th century. The exterior buttresses protrude also on the inner wall and are used as supports for ten transverse arches which span the interior. Above them lies an open wooden roof. The church with transverse arches is particularly widespread in Umbria, so much so that it could almost be claimed as an Umbrian speciality. (Further examples can be found in Piediluco, San Gemini, in Santa Maria di Monteluco at Perugia, in San Niccolo at Todi – but they are most common in Gubbio itself where nearly all the churches have transverse arches: San Giovanni, Sant' Agostino – both late 13th-century – San Pietro and San Domenico, from the 14th century.)

The transverse arch came to Umbria as a feature of Cistercian architecture. The monks of the order roofed their churches with vaults, but they used this arch for the large halls of their monastic buildings such as refectories and sick-rooms. Clearly the mendicant orders with their ideal of poverty were attracted by the austerity of this architectonic device, for they adopted the transverse-arched church in the second half of the 13th century.

48 GUBBIO Inner courtyard of the Palazzo Ducale. When the inhabitants of Gubbio realised that they could only escape having the bishop as master of the town by putting themselves under the protection of Montefeltre, the lord of Urbino, they chose the latter as the lesser of the two evils. It was the great Federico, born in Gubbio, who first commissioned the building of a ducal palace. He gave the work to the artists who had been engaged for more than a decade on the construction of the Residence at Urbino. Thus the Palazzo Ducale in Gubbio is only a younger brother of the palace at Urbino and, like it, remained unfinished. It is built of the same materials and their special properties are used in the same way. Once again the Dalmatian architect, Luciano da Laurana, has contrived to conjure forth the most wonderful and delicate play of colour from the contrast between the pilasters and articulation in *pietra serena* and the soft pink of the exquisite brick background. The detail on capitals and cornices is as fine as at Urbino. The courtyard is only cloistered on three sides, the upper storey on the fourth side being supported by a pronounced mediaeval corbel-table.

49 GUBBIO Wine-press of the cathedral chapter.
The chapter, which still owns 24 large properties, makes its own wine and stores it in large barrels. The wine-press dates from the 18th century at the latest. The original beam of the press, still in existence, extends to the full length of the cellar and is raised up and down on a threaded vertical pole turned by two men pushing a cross-bar capstan-fashion.

50 GUBBIO Via Galeotti.
Mediaeval alley in which the houses on both sides are linked by transverse arches, barrel vaults, etc.

51 Farmstead in the neighbourhood of GUBBIO.
Umbrian farmers frequently use the lower branches of trees for ripening corn-cobs in the sun, instead of the flat roofs of barns and stables as is usual in the rest of Italy. Hence the colourful 'corn-cob' trees whose golden-yellow fruits look quite exotic as they hang down among the greenery.

52 Farmland between Gubbio and Gualdo Tedino.
Typical sandstone country with its hills gently moulded by weathering.

53 Montefeltro and Monte Catria. The contrast between the smooth shapes of the sandstone hills and the shard contours of the towering limestone masses of Monte Catria (5,532 feet) in the High Apennines is particularly well brought out in this photograph, taken in the clear light of early spring.

54 URBINO   The ducal palace from the west.
Urbino's history is singularly uneventful. It first acquired a name in 1234 when, with the approval of the imperial authorities, the counts of Montefeltre became its rulers. By the 15th century they could no longer be called upstarts like the Medici in Florence or the Sforza in Milan; they were an ancient noble family which had already been ruling for more than two centuries. Greatest of the line was Duke Federico who ruled from 1444–82 and transformed Urbino into a 'Bethlehem in Judaea'.

To the left can be seen the rear of the cathedral, to the right the rear of the ducal palace. From the 15th century onwards they formed a unified group of buildings until the cathedral, begun in 1447, was so severely damaged by an earthquake in 1789 that it had to be replaced by a new building which, like the Renaissance structure consecrated in 1534, was topped by an octagonal drum surmounted in its turn by a dome. The two wings of the palace are separated towards the west by a central structure flanked by two slender stairway turrets; the structure's central axis is marked by a three-storeyed loggia. When it was first built, both the rear and the front of the palace facing the town were crowned with Gothic battlements instead of the existing roofs. To the left of the loggia, behind a high wall, the *giardino pensile*.

Below the loggia, the *Teatro Sanzio* (19th century) projects into the valley; to its right a section of the 15th-century town wall.

55 URBINO   The cathedral seen from the ducal palace.
The holes in the fabric show that the brickwork was meant to be faced with travertine blocks, as was actually done on the sides of the main doorway on the ground floor. The plain window framing with its semicircular top indicates that this east wing was erected before the advent of Luciano da Laurana. Behind this façade the master later installed the big double flight of steps in the corner of the palace.

56 URBINO   Ducal palace: the loggia flanked by the two stairway towers. One of the turrets has a spiral staircase with 130 steps. Their design is adopted from mediaeval defensive architecture, as indeed are the whole proportions of the sections facing the valley, which are entirely Gothic. The original battlements, now replaced by gutter-cornices, must have made the palace appear much more Gothic. This wing is certainly by the Dalmatian architect Luciano da Laurana who was appointed chief architect to the duke in 1468. As he had previously worked for René of Anjou on the castles of Villeneuve-les-Avignon and Tarascon, he was commissioned to build southern French round towers on many ecclesiastical and lay buildings in Italy.

57 URBINO The large inner courtyard of the ducal palace. The materials – *pietra serena* and pink brick – and the surface articulation are almost identical with the courtyard of the palace at Gubbio (see plate 48). Laurana was the architect in both cases. The plan of the courtyard is not quite square; it has five arcades on its north and south sides and six on the other two. But as the distance between the pillars varies, the overall effect is square nevertheless. There are continuous inscriptions (undated) lauding the proprietor on the friezes above both storeys. The recessed storey is one of the additions made to the palace by Girolama Genga in about 1536.

58 URBINO Ducal palace: the stairway.
It was not until the 15th century that Italy made the advance from the mediaeval spiral staircase to the straight flights of the new era. Even in the 15th century only one type of staircase, apart from the spiral, was known: a flight of stairs rising between two walls with barrel-vault roofing to a half-landing, followed by a flight running in the opposite direction. The exquisite decoration on the pilasters on the half-landing is attributed to Ambrogio Barocci, who was active in Urbino before 1479.

59 Agostino di Duccio: fragment of a marble relief showing a female head. Urbino, ducal palace (Galleria Nazionale delle Marche). See plates 16–17.

23 View of San Francesco from the citadel of Assisi

24 Spring in the Tescio valley, with Assisi in the background

25 Assisi. San Francesco

26 Assisi. San Francesco: apse

27   Assisi. San Francesco: the Piazza Inferiore

28 Assisi. The lower church of San Francesco: St Francis   29 Assisi. The upper church: from the Legend of St Francis

30   Assisi. The façade of Santa Chiara

31   Assisi. The Cathedral of San Rufino: the right-hand side doorway

32 Assisi. The Cathedral of San Rufino

33 Assisi. The Temple of Minerva

34   Assisi. View from the castle hill

35 The Tiber valley near Deruta

37   Pietro Perugino: portrait of a youth

38 Deruta. Pilgrimage church of Madonna di Bagno

41 The vale of Gubbio   42 Looking down on Gubbio

43   Gubbio. Palazzo dei Consoli and Palazzo Pretorio

44 Gubbio. The arched substructures

45   Gubbio. Alley with "doors of the dead"

46 The Feast of the Ceri in Gubbio

47   Gubbio. Interior of the Cathedral

48 Gubbio. Inner courtyard of the Palazzo Ducale

49   Gubbio. Wine-press of the Cathedral Chapter

50 Gubbio. Via Galeotti

51 Farmstead in the neighbourhood of Gubbio

52 Cultivated land between Gubbio and Gualdo Tadino

53   Montefeltro with Monte Catria beyond

54 Urbino. The ducal palace

55 Urbino. The Cathedral seen from the ducal palace

56   Urbino. Ducal palace: the loggia flanked by the two stairway towers

57 Urbino. The large inner courtyard of the ducal palace

58   Urbino. Ducal palace: the stairway

59 Agostino di Duccio: fragment of a relief

60 Federico da Montefeltre, Duke of Urbino. Urbino, ducal palace (Galleria Nazionale delle Marche).

Fifteenth-century relief in painted stucco. Since the famous double portrait of the Duke and his wife by Piero della Francesca in the Uffizi must have been painted about 1465, this relief must date from 1475 at the earliest, and probably depicts the Duke in his middle fifties. His nose was not naturally hooked but became so as the result of a wound received in battle.

Whereas philosophy was the main interest of the circle of the Medici in Florence, the court at Urbino was preoccupied with mathematical and scientific problems, especially optics. Piero della Francesca and the mathematician Fra Luca Pacioli were the leading lights. The Duke emanated a genuine magic: 'Feeling secure in a land where all gained profit or employment from his rule, and where none were beggars, he habitually went unaccompanied; alone among the princes of his time he ventured to walk in an open park, and to take his frugal meals in an open chamber, while Livy's history or (during Lent) some devotional work was read to him. Within a single afternoon he would attend a lecture on some classical subject, and visit the convent of the Order of St Clare to talk of sacred things with the abbess. In the evening he would watch the martial exercises of the young people of his Court in the meadow of San Francesco, famed for its magnificent view, and see to it well that all the feats were done in the most perfect manner. He strove always to be affable and accessible to the utmost degree, visiting the artisans who worked for him in their shops, holding frequent audiences, and, if possible, attending to the requests of each individual on the very day that they were presented. No wonder that the people as he walked along the street knelt down and cried: "Dio ti mantegna, Signore!" He earned the name of "the light of Italy".' (Jacob Burckhardt).

61 Raphael: *Sposalizio* (Milan, Brera). Wood, 46″ × 66½″. Urbino does not possess a single painting by its most famous son, Raphael, born here in 1483. (The portrait of a noble woman in the *galleria* of the ducal palace is only on loan from Florence and in any case is not an authenticated Raphael.) This picture was painted when Raphael was twenty-one and was commissioned for the church of San Francesco in Città di Castello; it is signed *Raphael Urbinas MDIIII*. It was painted in Umbria shortly before Raphael moved to Florence. The panel is still a genuine product of the Early Renaissance which Raphael was soon to leave far behind him. His palette and portrayal of people betray the pupil of Perugino, while the background shows the typically Umbrian predilection for centrally planned buildings. The picture was

painted in very close association with Perugino's picture of the same subject of 1503, now in the museum at Caen.

62 Joos van Gent: *The Communion of the Apostles* (detail). Urbino, ducal palace (Galleria Nazionale delle Marche). Wood, 121¼" × 131". This picture was painted for the Corpus Domini brethren in Urbino in 1473–74 by the Dutch painter Joos van Wassenhove, who moved to Italy about 1468 and from 1473 onwards was in the service of the court of Urbino, where he was known as Joos van Gent. The Duke is supposed to have summoned him because he wanted his palace decorated with paintings executed in the Dutch manner.

In this picture the northern painter had to adapt his art to the monumental scale preferred in the southern countries – 'it was difficult to reconcile the concentrated luminosity, which was achieved by layers of thin glazes, with the striving for a monumental effect.' (Max J. Friedländer). Undoubtedly the clumsy posture of Christ breaking the bread and the strained positions of the kneeling apostles who appear to have no solidity must have struck the Italians as peculiar. On the right, although he did not in fact commission the picture, is Federico da Montefeltre with two courtiers.

63 View from the SCHEGGIA Pass towards Monte Catria.
This comparatively low pass (2,054 feet) is both the most important and the easiest means of communication between Umbria and the Marches. The Via Flaminia, running from Foligno via Nocera and Gubbio, enters the Marches here. For over 2,000 years this road had no rival, then the railway was built, and another road through the pass, which had already been in use for many years, became more important. It branches off from the Via Flaminia shortly after Gualdo Tedino and leads over the Colle di Fossato (2,405 feet) to Fabriano. The Scheggia Pass only regained its importance with the improvement of road transport.

64 The vale between Fossato di Vico and Gualdo Tedino.
In the clear early spring light, with the last of the fresh snow on the peaks and heavy shadows on the hillsides, the Umbrian landscape takes on a heroic character, rather reminiscent of Greece (the Argolis, for example).

65 Trees such as the sweet chestnut, mulberry and hornbeam grow plentifully on the lower hills and in many of the basins and valleys between the Umbrian mountains.

66 Washing- and cattle-trough. One of the features common to the landscapes of both Umbria and Tuscany is the breed of white oxen with large curved horns. Used in teams for ploughing or to pull carts, they are part and parcel of the Umbrian land-scape. Bevagna, for example, was already famous in antiquity for the breed of oxen raised there.

67 NOCERA UMBRA   This town, once the seat of the bishopric, sprawls over the upper slope of a hillside with the cathedral on its summit, next to the ruins of a *rocca*. As long ago as classical times a road leading to Ancona branched off here from the Via Flaminia.

Unfortunately no classical remains or inscriptions have survived to the present day. The poplars in the middle of the photograph have been pollarded, i.e. their trunks have been stripped of foliage up to the very top. The foliage is then used as fodder, a practice also common in the Po valley.

68 SPELLO   Porta Venere. Spello lies on the southern spur of Monte Subasio and extends up the hillside. The town had to be more strongly fortified on the side facing the treeless massif than on that facing the plain, because it was most vulnerable to attack from above. This explains why the ancient Porta Venere, dating from the Augustan period, is a double fortification with an inner and an outer gate. The outer gate consists of a large central arch flanked by two smaller openings. There is a magnificent dodecagonal defence tower on either side of the gate. The inner lower section consists of a triple gate of which only one part is still standing.

69 Pinturicchio: *The Annunciation*. Fresco in the Capella Baglioni in Santa Maria Maggiore at Spello.
From 1425 Spello was in the hands of the lords of Perugia, the Baglioni, who maintained a garrison there. In addition a member of the family was usually in residence. Exactly twelve months after the end of 1500, a disastrous year when all the members of the house were murdered in a conspiracy (except Gian Paolo, who escaped), this chapel was painted with scenes from the life of Mary and the childhood of Christ by Pinturicchio, who had been commissioned by the Baglioni. *The Annunciation* is on the left-hand side wall. The contrast between the peaceful theme of the picture and the gruesome events which took place in the house of the man who commissioned it could scarcely be greater. The composition – a view of an open landscape, looking out from a columned hall and through an arcade – follows an old formula handed down to his pupils by Perugino.

In characteristically Early Renaissance style the figures are still concentrated in the foreground and, as it were, on the surface of the picture. There is little feeling of space around them; painted columns suffice as a formal background.

70 View of the Pianura from the slope below Montefalco. The hills forming the spurs of the Northern Apennines in the background of the picture are nearly all over 4,200 feet high. If the picture was extended, Monte Subasio would be the next mountain on the left. Foligno is a fast-growing industrial town which now stretches far out over the plain but has preserved the regular Roman street lay-out of its town centre virtually unchanged. This includes the quarter around the cathedral, an Early Christian foundation by Bishop Felician the Martyr, (about 250 BC), which stands out clearly.

Foligno was Umbria's most important road junction in antiquity and the Middle Ages and is now a railway junction.

71 FOLIGNO Santa Maria Infraportas.
The church was built in the 12th century just inside the town walls and near the western gate. Originally consisting of a single low barrel-vaulted nave, it was converted into a three-aisled church in the 15th century. The portico in front of the façade also dates from the 12th century.

72-4 FOLIGNO The Cathedral. The façade of the northern transept was treated elaborately because it faced the piazza. (The interior has been completely restyled in the Baroque manner.) The façade was begun by the two masters Rudolphus and Binellus, who were also responsible for the two churches in the piazza at Bevagna and their Latin inscriptions (see plates 76–77). The two artists' contribution ends above the rose windows of the side panels. The Gothic bifora of the third storey were added in the early 15th century. Unfortunately the large rose windows and the gable were clumsily restored in 1905. On the upper part of the columns on the portal are full-length figures in relief representing Emperor Frederick Barbarossa (or Henry IV) and Bishop Anselm, the Bishop with his hand raised in benediction. The then Ghibelline town had every reason to keep Barbarossa's memory alive, because the Emperor promised Bevagna and Corcurione (now Montefalco) to Foligno in a privilege dated 1184.

75 FOLIGNO Frescoes in the Palazzo Trinci. The Trinci were the ruling family of Foligno who rose to power as leaders of the Guelph faction and were able to legitimise their domination after 1310 when Rinaldo Trinci became a Papal vicar. The family then remained continuously in power until 1439 and managed, under the celebrated Niccolo Trinci who assumed command in 1420, to establish a large principality which included Spello, Assisi, Bevagna, Montefalco, Trevi and Nocera. It was also the time of the town's great cultural flowering. The family palace of the Trinci lies immediately in the shadow of the cathedral, on the narrow side of the square. Whereas the town palaces of the other signorial families were without exception destroyed as acts of vengeance by their enemies (the Baglioni palace at Perugia was razed to the ground after the capture of the town by Pope Paul III) the fresco cycles in the Palazzo Trinci remain, the only evidence left of the outlook of courtly society during the transition from the late Middle Ages to the Early Renaissance. The palace was completed in 1407. Its halls are decorated with cycles of the nine heroes of Roman history, the liberal arts and the planets, painted in 1424 by Ottavio Nelli and other Umbrian masters who had studied in a northern Italian school.

76 BEVAGNA Palazzo dei Consoli. Bevagna, the Roman *municipium* of Mevania, lies on the stretch of the Via Flaminia which was abandoned in the early Middle Ages. But the character of the town today is entirely late mediaeval. The piazza is one of

the most impressive town squares in Umbria. The fountain is actually neo-Gothic (1889), but the Palazzo dei Consoli itself was built about 1270, although it has been somewhat too pedantically restored. On the long sides of the square the two late Romanesque churches of San Silvestro and San Michele face each other, the first built, according to the inscription, by Master Binellus in 1195, the second by Binellus in collaboration with another artist.

77 BEVAGNA   San Michele: part of the springing-stone of the left-hand main doorway.

78 BEVAGNA   The crypt of San Michele. The inscription reads: *Rodulfus et Binellus fecer(unt) hec opera. Christus benedicat il(l)os senper et Michael custodiat.* Above it is a relief showing the church's patron, the Archangel Michael, fighting the dragon. The whole doorway with a Cosmatesque frieze as its outermost archivolt has strong affinities with another work by the two masters, the doorway of the transept of Foligno Cathedral (see plate 74). The crypt seems spacious because the presbytery is placed very high and finished with a semi-circular apse. Some of the pillars were taken from classical buildings. The whole is roofed in by cross-vaulting running between narrow transverse ribs.

79 Roman floor-mosaic at BEVAGNA   A Roman mosaic of the 2nd century AD was discovered in a private house near the town's north-western exit. It measures 39 ft by 21 ft 8 ins and is entirely composed of black and white stones. The composition is arranged in two sections; in the upper one a triton hunts a sea-horse, in the lower are two leaping dolphins and other creatures (mostly destroyed), in addition to the lobster shown here.

80 BEVAGNA   City wall. The mediaeval walls, of which about 1¼ miles are in a good state of preservation, date from between 1249 and 1377. Part of the building was on the top of the Roman walls; and sections of wall were increased in height at a later date. Square, cylindrical or polygonal towers project from the wall, in which there are five gates. Remains of the antique town walls in squared and diamond-shaped stone (mentioned by Pliny) have also been preserved.

81 BEVAGNA   Public wash-house by the Clitunno.

82 The Torre de Montefalco with the Teverone bridge between Montefalco and Foligno.
This tower and bridge have survived from the 14th century. The tower was to be used for defence purposes.

83 MONTEFALCO seen from the Pianura. Whereas all the other hill towns lie on the slopes above the eastern edge of the Pianura (Spoleto, Trevi, Spello, Assisi), Montefalco, on a tongue-shaped ridge, sticks out into the plain on the western side.

Its unique situation has given the town the nickname of the *ringhiera dell' Umbria* (the balcony with a view of Umbria).

84 The Pianura and Monte Subasio seen from Trevi. The town on the plain at the foot of Monte Subasio is Foligno.

85 MONTEFALCO Fresco in the Cappella Santa Croce in Santa Chiara.
The importance of this little town lies in its past history: it is now very quiet, even insignificant. Nevertheless in times past eight saints made it their home, for which reason it is now celebrated as *un lembo di cielo caduto in terra* (a piece of heaven which has fallen down to earth). The interiors of the town's churches are decorated with mediaeval frescoes, the most famous of which (by the Florentine Early Renaissance painter Benozzo Gozzoli) is in the choir of San Francesco and depicts the life of St Francis (1450–52). This photograph shows a fresco of the crucifixion by an unknown master; it was painted in 1333 and is now in the Cappella Santa Croce of Santa Chiara. It is undoubtedly the work of an Umbrian painter but one who had been influenced by the Sienese school. He was evidently familiar with both the crucifixion fresco by Pietro Lorenzetti and the big painted crucifix by Giotto. The founder of the chapel is shown on a reduced scale kneeling to the right of the stem of the cross; he is portrayed wearing contemporary clothes and an ermine collar, in order further to distinguish him from the characters in the main drama. This is one of the very rare crucifixion pictures in which John, the favourite disciple, is kneeling instead of standing, as he mourns.

86 Alleyway in Trevi, showing the cobbled steps and the walls of irregular dressed stones so often encountered in Umbrian towns and villages.

87 FONTI DEL CLITUNNO The poplars clustering round the sources of the Clitumnus. In a letter to a correspondent of the Emperor Trajan, Pliny the Younger (who died about 114 BC) asks: 'Have you ever seen the Clitumnus? A spring flows from a cypress-shaded hill in several channels which then unite to form a broad pool. The water is so clear and pure that you can count the votive coins and shining pebbles on the bottom. On its banks stand ash trees and alders whose reflections seem deeply embedded in the stream. The water is as cold as snow. An old temple stands nearby; in it lives the god Clitumnus; the oracles say that he is gracious and knows our destinies. Small temples stand on the minor tributaries which later all flow into the main body of the river.'
The temples have disappeared since then but otherwise this grove on the Via Flaminia, 5½ miles north of Spoleto, has changed little since the time of Pliny's description. Today the sources form a very shallow lake out of which the Clitumnus flows. It then runs parallel with the Maroggia and, like it, joins the Timia near Bevagna. The lovely slender poplars still stand as in Pliny's day and the water is still transparent and cold as snow.

It was in 1876 when Giosuè Carducci was inspector of schools in Spoleto that he wrote the famous poem *To the Sources of the Clitumnus*, included in the *Odi barbare*.

88 Temple above the Clitumnus, near Trevi. When Pliny wrote his letter, the Temple of Clitumnus, about half a mile northwards close to the Via Flaminia, had not been built; it was erected in the 5th century AD. Presumably in those days the Clitumnus flowed straight past the front of the temple. It is a beautifully-proportioned building, in a wonderful state of preservation. The frieze on the front bears the inscription: *Sanctus Deus Angelorum qui fecit resurrectionem*, indicating that this building, like so many Early Christian churches, was dedicated to Our Saviour. Everything about the temple is unusual. A wide variety of materials were used in its construction; the pilasters and their capitals of the façade are marble but all the rest is limestone, while the sides are faced with slightly-irregular travertine blocks. Only the left-hand one of the two voluted pillars on the façade is monolithic, the other being composed of several drums of different heights. The capitals of columns and pillars do not match in the least; there is a gap between the entablatures of front and side walls so that these, too, present a rather irregular appearance. The temple's design is as unusual as its technical details. In the classical period this type of temple – with tetrastyle in antis – never had additional supports next to the pillars on the side walls of the cella which are nearest the front; thus, strictly speaking, the voluted columns are superfluous. But it is by no means certain, as some people claim, that they were only added later to strengthen the building.

The little temple was probably built in the second half of the 5th century but even then as a Christian church. The fact that the semi-circular termination to the cella is original supports this theory. So does the inscription. The barrel vaulting of the cella and the vestibule of limestone and brick, on the other hand, date from an early mediaeval restoration. It is obvious that in the 5th century material for the Christian sanctuary was taken from the pagan temples which, according to Pliny, stood near the source of the Clitumnus, but which were no longer used for pagan rites by this date and had consequently fallen into ruin.

89 SPOLETO from the south-west. Spoleto is now the most important strong point in Italy, although this has not always been the case. Founded as a Latin colony in 241 BC, it was at first only celebrated for its geographied situation dominating the southern part of the Pianura. This remained the case until post-Tiberian times when the Via Flaminia was rebuilt; then a main road passed through Interamnia (Terni) and Spoleto, while a secondary road linked the town with the Via Salaria and the Adriatic coast via Norcia and Arquato del Tronco. The town was already playing an important part in Italian affairs during Gothic times, and Theodoric embellished it with buildings. Immediately after the Lombard conquest in 569 Spoleto became the capital of a dukedom which controlled a large area of central Italy.

On the castle hill are remains of walls in polygonal style; the existing *rocca* was constructed after 1354 when the town had been recaptured for the Church by the Spanish Cardinal Albornoz. From 1362 onwards the building operations were directed by the architect Gattapone of Gubbio, who had erected a wonderful group of public buildings in his own town (see plates 39–41). The *rocca* has a regular rectangular plan with six towers and is divided into two roughly-square enclosures by a horizontal wing. The block facing the town housed the garrison, the upper one served as the governor's residence.

On the right, the Ponte delle Torri.

90 SPOLETO   Ponte delle Torri. This aqueduct, which spans the deep gorge between the castle hill and the slope of Monte Luco, is a brick structure with ten arches; it is 670 feet long and 264 feet high. It both supplied the garrison of the citadel with water and served as a bridge. In its present-day form it dates from the Gothic period, as the pointed arches of its arcades clearly show; it was, in fact, built at the same time as the *rocca*, on Cardinal Albornoz's orders. Consequently the theory has been put forward that Gattapone of Gubbio was the architect in both cases, since castle and aqueduct would naturally form a single architectural undertaking. However there is a good deal of evidence to support the theory that the Lombards had already spanned the gorge with an aqueduct soon after 604 and that Cardinal Albornoz only had it enlarged and extended.

At the end of the aqueduct facing Monte Luco is a fortified bridge-head in the form of a small castle.

91 SPOLETO   The Cathedral. The cathedral lies on a terrace near the top of the hill on which the town is built, but below the castle. The façade, like those of so many Umbrian buildings, is characterised by a severely-plain surface, with only two narrow arcades and a virtual absence of articulation by mouldings or reliefs. Although the interior of the cathedral is now Baroque, its façade is still part of the original building which the great Pope Innocent III consecrated in 1198. Admittedly the exterior was probably still unfinished at that time but the façade so closely resembles those of Assisi Cathedral and San Pietro at Spoleto, known to date from about 1200 (see plates 32, 98), that there can be little doubt as to its date. On the upper part of the façade is a mosaic – a similar work was originally intended to occupy the same place on San Pietro outside the town. It shows Christ, His hand raised in blessing, between the Virgin Mary and St John, and is signed with the name Solsterno and the date 1207.

The lovely Renaissance portico was added to the façade in 1491. It is the work of Ambrogio da Milano and Pippo di Antonio da Firenze. The campanile is 12th century, but the attractive belfry was not added until the Early Renaissance and the steeple only in 1518. The Late Romanesque and Early Renaissance sections of the building combine surprisingly well.

92 SPOLETO   The cathedral: fresco by Pinturicchio in the Cappella Eroli.
The first chapel on the right-hand side of the nave was painted by Pinturicchio who was commissioned by Bishop Costantino Eroli. The painting shows the Madonna enthroned with the Child.

93 SPOLETO   Sant' Eufemia. Today this little church, which seems hardly more than a chapel, forms part of the group of buildings which make up the archbishop's palace. Originally it may well have replaced the chapel of the ducal palace. In spite of its small proportions it must be considered the most interesting, if not the most important, late mediaeval church in Umbria. It is unique in Umbria for its internal design – three-aisled structure with a gallery – and for the perpendicular emphasis of its proportions. One may assume from the fact that San Lorenzo, Verona, its mother church, was completed in 1110, that Sant'Eufemia dates from the same period. Although the small shafts in front of the wall of the main aisle are original it is doubtful whether the roof was meant to be vaulted; the vaulting now to be seen is modern. The original roof was probably of wood and supported by flying-buttresses, like that of San Lorenzo in Verona. Much of the material used in the capitals and pillars was looted from other churches; many of the capitals are in a Byzantine style.

94 SPOLETO   San Salvatore, presbytery. Spoleto owes its unique position in the history of Italian Early Christian architecture to this church which is situated outside the town. The three-aisled basilica of San Salvatore was built at the end of the 4th or the beginning of the 5th century. Fire and other catastrophes did little damage to the façade, but they so affected the interior of the nave that the intercolumniation, which originally had a smooth architrave and a frieze with triglyphs, had to be walled in long ago. But fortunately the ancient splendour of the late classical structure with its sculptural weight and luxuriant decoration have been preserved in the presbytery. The question of how the church was roofed remains rather obscure. A flat wooden roof and cross-vaulting have both been suggested. (The existing dome over the crossing dates from the 18th century). Neither the façade nor the eastern end of the church conform completely to the style of the Early Christian architecture of Rome (or for that matter of the rest of Italy). The influence of eastern Early Christian architecture, especially Syrian, led, for example, to the eastern apse being placed between two pastophoria and the curve of the apse being faced with a flat wall on the outside.

95 SPOLETO   San Domenico, fresco of the *Pietà*.
Pietà pictures were introduced into Central Italy by travelling German artists, and nowhere was the new idea more avidly welcomed than in Umbria. Not only were the local wood-carvers quick to adopt it but local painters also soon added it to their repertoire. The painted image of the Virgin on the north wall of the church of San Domenico probably dates from about 1440.

96 The fact that the Church of San Pietro in Valle stands outside the town gate implies that it is a memorial built over a necropolis, and a burial field did in fact exist here from the Iron Age until the Early Christian epoch.

97, 98 San Pietro in Valle. Façade.
The church was dedicated to St Peter at the beginning of the 5th century after it had acquired, through the agency of Bishop Achilles, a relic from the saint's chain. The interior is wholly Baroque but the façade is the most important example of Romanesque architecture in Umbria to be decorated with reliefs and sculptures. The division into panels, by broad pilasters, of a surface deliberately kept very flat, is exactly like that on the façade of Assisi Cathedral; the horizontal mouldings of the Assisi panels present a similar appearance. Moreover, at Assisi too the doorways are flanked by figures of animals which look as though they were meant to serve as pedestals but in fact have no columns on them. Again the façades of both churches have griffins projecting below the first moulding. The façade of San Pietro in Valle, like that of Assisi, dates from about 1200. The exquisite decorative foliage which runs continuously round the jambs and lintel of the main portal was adopted from the late classical façade of San Salvatore where it appears on all three lintels above the west portals. These leaves also appear on the Late Romanesque main doorway of the cathedral. The voluted columns with regular rhythmic spirals are common in the work of the Cosmati at Rome.
   The iconographic subject-matter is not easy to interpret. The reliefs immediately flanking the centre door consist of three sets of identical pairs – the bottom pair showing a farmer with a team of oxen and his dog, the pair above a doe feeding its young while it kills a snake; and the pair above that again a peacock eating grapes; the last subject is a familiar symbol in Early Christian art. The rectangular panels framing these reliefs are filled with scenes of animals fighting and struggles between men and monsters. The two topmost panels are by a different artist from the rest. The relief work is flatter and the subject-matter definitely Christian: Christ washing Peter's feet, Christ calming the waters of Lake Tiberias, the death of the righteous man and the death of the sinner. The symbols of the four evangelists are placed at intervals round the rose window on the middle storey. The central panel on the third storey, now bricked up, was probably originally intended to contain a mosaic. On either side of this empty space are two angels with censers and two bulls looking down, all four by the master who was responsible for the scenes from the life of Christ. In the same decade similar bulls, sculptured in the round, were added to the decoration of the top storey of the tower of Laon Cathedral in France. Above the two side doors are St Michael fighting the dragon and a canonised bishop. The volutes on the third storey date from the 16th century.

99 The Corno valley near TRIPONZO   The Corno is a minor tributary of the Nera with its source in the Reatine hills. It flows northward and joins the Nera near Triponzo. This section of the Corno valley shows part of the road from Spoleto to

Norcia. The river has bitten its way deep into the valley in comparatively recent times, as its steeply-sloping and sharply-defined banks show.

100 NORCIA the native town of St Benedict (born AD 480), lies in a fertile basin encircled by hills. The surrounding land, marshy and dotted with pools and springs, is watered by the Sordo. The town itself is situated on a low plateau above this damp ground, and has never spread beyond the confines of its 14th-century town wall. Norcia has suffered numerous earthquakes (the last big one in 1859) which explains why the towers and palaces to be seen above its wall are not more thickly clustered. According to the building regulations established after the last earthquake houses were not to exceed 40 feet in height.

Norcia is famous for its sausages. Throughout Sabina and even in Rome itself there are specialist pork butchers' shops called *Norcerina*.

101 MONTE VETTORE (8,053 feet) above the Forca Canapine. The Forca Canapine (5,015 feet) is the watershed between the Tyrrhenian and Adriatic seas, and also the boundary between Umbria and the Marches. The limestone mass of the Monte Vettore, with its jagged edges, is the southernmost peak of the Monte Sibillini. This photograph shows the west side of the barren massif. The eastern slope where the bare rock lies exposed is particularly impressive.

102 ASCOLI-PICENO from the north. Built on a plateau at the junction of the rivers Tronto and Castellano, which flow round it on either side, Ascoli-Piceno is probably the most important town in the Marches after Ancona and Macerata. It owes its historical importance to its site at the emergence of the Via Salaria from the mountains. This road runs down the narrow gorge-like valley of the Tronto and crosses the last of the numerous narrow passes via the Gola of Acquasanta. South of the Scheggia Pass, the Tronto valley forms the first important west-east line of communication between Rome and the Adriatic coast. The town was fully conscious of its key position in ancient times and in fact Italian rebellion against Rome in 90 BC began here. The only reason that the town has not played a more important part in recent Italian history is that the political, cultural and economical life of the peninsula has increasingly become concentrated along the Tyrrhenian coast.

In the foreground the deep Tronto valley; above it the Ponte di Solestà across which the Via Salaria enters the town. The bridge consists of a single arch and was built in early imperial times. On the south bank, the mediaeval town gate, the Porta Solestà (1230); behind it, several watch towers.

103 ASCOLI-PICENO   Renaissance arcades, with public buildings above, make three sides of the Piazza del Popolo.

104 ASCOLI-PICENO   Piazza del Popolo, with San Francesco. Like most of the town's churches, the church of San Francesco is now a hall church with three aisles of equal

height. The nave was consecrated in 1371, but the choir was not begun until 1460 (completed in 1464). The vaulting was first introduced in 1567 but even before this the open rafters of the three aisles presented a very unified appearance. But the unforgettable feature of San Francesco is the choir. The transept and choir are completely surrounded by seven chapels or apsidoles. From the outside there appear to be nine bays, seven of which are these chapels while the other two are the lower sections of the two towers. The windows with their pointed arches, the slender responds surging upwards at the corners of the polygonal apsidioles and lastly the two towers of the choir rising high above the gutter cornice, all show the thoroughly Gothic outlook which still prevailed here around 1460. The dome over the crossing, added in the 16th century, has not really succeeded in counteracting the effect of this vertical emphasis. The Piazza del Popolo, surrounded on three sides by Renaissance arcades, is one of the loveliest enclosed squares in the whole of Italy.

105 ASCOLI-PICENO   SS. Vicenzo e Anastasia.
The unfinished façade divided into 64 panels is very reminiscent of the flat Umbrian façade of Assisi cathedral or San Pietro in Valle at Spoleto but, owing to Ascoli's provincial isolation, it was not built until nearly 200 years later (1389). The main doorway which formed part of the original single-naved church dates from the beginning of the 14th century (see the doorway of the Palazzo dei Priori in Perugia, plate 11), but the façade as it now stands – that is, divided into panels – was only added when two further aisles were built on to the church. On the tympanum, the Madonna and Child, with the two patron saints of the church on either side. The campanile dates from the 12th century.

60 Federico da Montefeltre, Duke of Urbino

61 Raphael: Sposalizio

62 Joos van Gent: The Communion of the Apostles

63 View from the Scheggia pass towards Monte Catria

64 The vale between Fossato di Vico and Gualdo Tadino

65 Sweet chestnut

66 Washing- and cattle-trough

67 Nocera Umbra

68 Spello. Porta Venere   69 Pinturicchio: The Annunciation

70 View of the Pianura from the slope below Montefalco

71 Foligno. Santa Maria Infraportas

72—73 Foligno. The Cathedral: doorway reliefs of Emperor and Bishop

74 Foligno. The Cathedral: lateral façade

75   Foligno. Frescoes in the Palazzo Trinci

76   Bevagna. Palazzo dei Consoli

77 Bevagna. San Michele: Part of the springing-stone of the left-hand main doorway

78 Bevagna. The crypt of San Michele

80 Bevagna. City wall

81　Bevagna. Public wash-house by the Clitunno

82 The Torre de Montefalco with the Teverone bridge

83 Montefalco seen from the Pianura

85 Montefalco. Fresco in Santa Chiara

86 Alleyway in Trevi

88 Temple above the Clitunno, near Trevi

89   Spoleto, from the south-west

90 Spoleto. Ponte delle Torri

91 Spoleto. The Cathedral

92   Spoleto. The Cathedral: fresco by Pinturicchio

93 Spoleto. Sant'Eufemia

94 Spoleto. San Salvatore

95   Spoleto. San Domenico: fresco of the Pietà

96 The Ticino valley with San Pietro in Valle, outside Spoleto

97—98 San Pietro in Valle. Façade

99 The Corno valley near Triponzo

100 Norcia

101 Monte Vettore   102 Ascoli-Piceno, from the nort

103   Ascoli-Piceno. The arcades of San Francesco

104 Ascoli-Piceno. Piazza del Popolo, with San Francesco

105   Ascoli-Piceno. SS. Vicenzo e Anastasio

106 View of the Apennino Marchipiano from above the Forca di Presto on Monte Vettore. Lower left centre: Arquata del Tronco perched on a ridge. Below this village the road out of Umbria from Norcia via Forca Canapine joins the Via Salaria. It is the most important line of communication between southern Umbria and the Adriatic coast. The photograph was taken from a height of 6,337 feet and gives a good idea of the open character of the magnificent mountain mass.

107 In this region there are both large nomadic droves of sheep, which usually winter in the Campagna near Rome, and flocks attached to specific localities and looked after by the local sheep farmers.

108 PIANOGRANDE DI MONTE VETTORE   The Pianogrande, 4½ miles long and 2½ miles broad, was originally a lake but this has long since dried up. Although in June it is covered with flowers and sweet-smelling herbs, in autumn the muddy brown and pale grey of its arid soil and its bare treeless slopes give it an almost Tibetan appearance. (This photograph was taken in early October.) Castelluccio, above the Piano, is one of the highest villages in the whole of Italy (4,722 feet). It has 800 inhabitants who possess between them some 2,000 sheep. Two or three centuries ago, before the Maremma plain was much cultivated, sheep-rearing was an even more important industry in this region. Consequently almost all the inhabitants are shepherds. Every evening the flocks are driven up to the village from the Pianogrande so that the young lambs, which are kept in pens, can be fed by their mothers. The Pianogrande is so solitary that in years gone by the Vatican decreed that it should not be crossed from November to March and that the bells of Castelluccio should ring continuously on misty or stormy days so that lost travellers could get their bearings.

109 PIANOGRANDE DI SANTA SCHOLASTICA ABOVE NORCIA   The fertile arable land stretching to the south of Norcia is named after St Benedict's sister. This late September photograph shows broad fields of stubble.

110, 111 San Pietro in Valle, near FERENTILLO
The monastery was founded by the Lombard Duke Faroald of Spoleto who himself entered it as a monk in 724 and later died there. But the church which now stands was not built until the 11th century. While the main aisle has a flat roof, the transepts on either side of the cross-vaulted crossing are roofed with barrel-vaulting. In this picture the church is in the centre and behind the other monastery buildings. The campanile also dates from the 11th century.

But in general this lonely monastery is celebrated not for its architecture but for the frescoes in the nave; these depict the story of the Creation, and of Adam and Eve from the moment when 'God said, Let there be light: and there was light'. The Old Testament subject-matter was, of course, used in many other Byzantine murals but these frescose are original in that they are looking away from the typically Eastern style and form, and aiming at a native Italian type of expression. They were painted in about 1200, the beginning of the century which was to see an ever increasing divergence between Western and Byzantine art, culminating in the splendid achievements of Giotto.

In front of the main altar is an antependium which dates from the time when the abbey was founded. It is the only important example of Lombard relief sculpture to have survived in Umbria. From its inscription – a dedication to Duke Hilderich of Spoleto – it is ascribed to about 739–40. Plate 110 shows the middle section, containing the oldest early mediaeval self-portrait known to exist. The stone-mason has portrayed himself as a man with a pointed beard and a chisel in his hand. The inscription runs '*Ursus magister fecit*' and in addition the antependium is decorated with a cross and other eucharistic symbols.

112 FERENTILLO with the gorge of the Nera.
The Fossa Salto del Cieco flows into the Nera here. The river divides the town into two parts, Precetto on the left and Materella on the right. Above both sections of the town, high up on the mountain side, are the ruins of castles which once barred the entrance to the Nera valley.

113 A peaceful scene outside one of Ferentillo's small *trattorie*.

114 Nitrogen works in the Nera valley, near Terni. Soon after Italy became a single kingdom, the government set up a large state-owned armaments factory here, and this is still in existence. In 1884 it was joined by a steel and smelting company, followed by a calcium-carbide company in 1899, and lastly an acetylene chemical firm. Because hydraulic power is used for the fission of metallic carbides, the waters of the Nera, the Corno, the Velino and Lake Piediluco have been artificially diverted and harnessed to serve the electro-chemical industry.

115 The Cascata delle Marmore in the Nera Valley. This waterfall is almost as famous as the Cascata de Tivoli but it can only be seen in its full glory on Sunday, because during the week it is used to provide power for the chemical industry. Another result of industrialisation is that the luxuriant green vegetation which used to surround the waterfall has receded year by year.

The waterfall is not a natural phenomenon, but was artificially created at the spot where the waters of the Velino fell into the Nera below. In 271 BC the Roman consul Manius Curtius Dentatus, noticing that the waters of the Velino were stagnating on the high plateau of Le Marmore, had a channel dug so that they were diverted to flow down over three separate terraces with a total height of 500 feet; it was, and still is, constantly supplied by the richly-watered basin of the Rieti. In the foreground the Terni-Ferentillo road.

116 THE LAKE OF PIEDILUCO and the Monti Reatini This is the biggest lake in Umbria after Lake Trasimeno. It lies 1,210 feet above sea level and has a maximum depth of 65 feet. Although the lake has managed to preserve the calm of its dark green and black surface and the peace of its shores, it plays an important part as the reservoir providing water power for the electro-chemical industries of the Terni basin. Since 1925 the lake has been connected with the Velino by an artificial canal which has replaced the natural outlet, a narrow, and cramped stream. Dominating the town of Piediluco on a hill top is a mediaeval *rocca*, which was built by Cardinal Albornoz in 1364.

117 View of the Terno basin, Papigno and Valnerina from Monte Sant' Angelo. PAPIGNO is the headquarters of the big *stabilimento elettrochimico* for the production of calcium carbide (not visible in this photograph). Centre right: the Nera Valley winds in an S-bend, with the Terni-Rieti railway running parallel to it. Terni itself is in the background of the picture behind the pylon on the left.

118 The bridge of Augustus near NARNI Built on the occasion of the re-opening of the Via Flaminia by Emperor Augustus. The bridge was once 420 feet long, with four arches, and first collapsed owing to flood water in the 7th or 8th century; it was repaired and was destroyed once again, this time irreparably, in 1054. Until 1885 half of a second pier was still standing in the river; it is reproduced in the famous painting by Corot in the Louvre (1826). The exceptional height of the bridge, 37 feet above water level, is due to the fact that Narni is a mountain village and that the Via Flaminia also runs along the slope of a mountain, the Monte Santa Croce, on the other side of the river. Procopius, a 6th-century Byzantine author, wrote: 'Of all the arches I have seen, this is the highest.'

Presumably there was a suburb near the bridge in the late classical period, especially since, from imperial times onward, the old branch of the Via Flaminia (leading to Carsulae and Bevagna) and the new stretch (to Interamnia-Terni) met here. In imperial times there was water-traffic from Narni to Rome. Previously the Nera had been considered unnavigable.

119 NARNI Fountain in the Piazza Communale.
In its construction the fountain is a simplified version of the Fontana Maggiore in the square at Perugia (see plate 7). It dispenses with the second stone basin, but otherwise the structure is similar. The lower basin is a polygon with short columns at the corners which stand on semicircular bases, each with three steps, and the water pipe and bowl are made of bronze, as in Perugia, but there is no relief work.

The Narni fountain is a generation older than the famous fountain by the Pisani family (1301). In addition there are several Gothic fountains in Narni.

120 NARNI   The Cathedral: chapel of SS. Giovenale and Cassio.

The front of this sacellum in the right-hand aisle is faced with marble panels which are divided up by 6th-century pilasters and mouldings. The door jambs and lintel are surrounded by a broad mosaic border in the Cosmatesque manner (late 13th to 14th century). The wrought-iron work is from the same period.

Later a relief was added above the lintel, of the type which was originally used for choir chests, ambos or other church furniture. It shows the Cross between two lambs. The detailed inscription was added later when the marble was used as a burial panel for St Cassius, the patron saint of Narni. The inscription bears no date, but the saint died in 558.

121 TODI   The Cathedral.

The far end of Todi's slightly sloping piazza is bordered by the cathedral. A Late Renaissance flight of steps leads up to the façade which was articulated in the 13th century. It is one of the usual homogeneous fronts divided into rectangular panels by pilasters and mouldings in the typical Umbrian tradition. In the 13th century the façade was probably intended to be surmounted by a broad triangular gable (see plate 32), but later the plain, flat roof must have so appealed to the new Renaissance sensibility that the idea of a gable was abandoned. Although the three doors have pointed arches, the form of the main doorway with its broad Late Romanesque frieze of foliage running round doorjambs and archivolt is markedly anti-gothic in feeling. The large rose window here was probably the inspiration for the great rose window on the façade of Orvieto Cathedral. The campanile at the side may also date from the 13th century.

122 TODI   Piazza del Popolo, with the Palazzi Comunali. The cathedral occupies one side of the square, while the town's public buildings form a group on the opposite side. On the extreme left and only partially visible in the photograph is the Palazzo del Capitano (begun in 1209). The platform on top of the broad flight of steps connects it with the Palazzo del Popolo, whose lower part, consisting of the open loggia and an upper storey, was built in 1213 but added to between 1228 and 1233. The Gothic battlements on the roof were restored in the 19th century. On the far right can be seen the windows of the Palazzo dei Priori, which was begun in 1293 and enlarged in 1334-37. In 1513 the windows of both storeys were transformed at the orders of Pope Leo X by the addition of lovely Renaissance frames. A tower (1369-85) surmounts the left-hand corner of this palace. The whole history of mediaeval Todi is reflected in this group of buildings. The town was made a free *comune* as early as the 12th century and reached the peak of its importance in the 13th and early 14th centuries. Todi joined the association of Guelph towns in Umbria in 1237 and put up a successful resistance against the Hohenstaufen

Emperor Frederick II in 1240. During the 14th century the town came under the dominion of various signorial families, of whom the Atti are the best known.

123 The Early Renaissance Florentine painter Domenico Ghirlandaio painted an altar panel showing the crowning of the Virgin in 1486, for the convent of San Girolamo at Nani.

124 Lo Spagna: *The Coronation of the Virgin* (detail).

Although large parts of Ghirlandaio's *Crowning of the Virgin* were executed by his assistants, the painting was so much admired in Umbria that Giovanni Spagna, a Spaniard studying under Perugino, was commissioned by the procurator of Monte Santo in Narni to make a copy of it for that church. (It was finished in 1511.) The difference between Florentine and Umbrian methods of characterisation and composition can be seen even in the black and white reproductions of these two pictures. Ghirlandaio is penetrating and realistic in his portrayal of men; like all the Florentine painters he is deeply preoccupied with physiognomy. Every line and wrinkle is faithfully reproduced. Lo Spagna's figures resemble each other more closely because they all have the same mild pious expression and most of them have that 'heaven-turned' gaze which is characteristic of the products of Perugino's workshop. Compare the two versions of the profile of St Louis of Toulouse (the bishop in the pluvial kneeling in the foreground with his back to the spectator). Ghirlandaio's profile is clean cut, as if he were making a design for a medal, and the front of the face is quite clearly differentiated from the temples; the details on the two points of the mitre are drawn with such precision and three-dimensional clarity that the pearl embroidery almost seems to stand out from the material. In the Umbrian's work the individual features of the profile merge with each other without definition, the front part of the face as a whole is on the same plane as the temples and ears, the mitre is a single shape rather than a collection of separate details. Whereas Ghirlandaio's coronation is painted on a gold background, Lo Spagna has substituted a soft open Umbrian landscape which makes an excellent foil for his kneeling worshippers and serves to distinguish the grey of the cloaks, the green-grey of the hills, the flesh tones and the rich ecclesiastical robes from one another. Ghirlandaio's colour contrasts were much too harsh for Umbrian eyes; the bright enclosed patches of colour on the robes of the figures kneeling in the foreground with their aggressive contrasts seemed far too abrupt to Lo Spagna's taste. He wanted gradations, transitional tones between these colours. So he turned St Louis' bright ultramarine cloak, which is decorated with the French *fleur de lys*, into a white pluvial with brocade patterns in soft grey. Deliberately avoiding the ruthlessly unambiguous quality of Ghirlandaio's painting, Lo Spagna also sacrificed much of his luminosity and intelligibility. Thus the subtle Florentine shimmering effects in the robes of the angels hovering round the coronation scene in two half choirs were far too nervous and refined for Umbrian tastes and Lo Spagna did not try to imitate them.

125 TODI   San Fortunato. The Vallombrosan monastery which was handed over to the Minorites in 1254 was a centre of the Fransiscan movement in Umbria during the second half of the 13th and 14th centuries. Fra Iacopone da Todi, the great lyric poet who died in 1307, belonged to the monastery for a short time.

The foundation stone of the three-aisled church was laid in 1292. The eastern part of the church was in use in 1328 but was only covered with a temporary roof. For a long time the two eastern bays were cut off from the section which had barely been started by a dividing wall. There was a long break in construction, then work was resumed with the two western piers in 1408. The vaulting was begun in 1458 and finished in 1463. The dividing wall between the 14th- and 15th-century structures was removed in 1464. In 1465 the church was completed. The nave has four bays; the outer walls of the two aisles have a row of low chapels along them. On top of the chapels is a gallery running parallel to the clerestory. The nave is twice the width of the side aisles which end in a flat wall, while the nave terminates in a polygonal choir forming seven sides of a dodecagon. The clustered columns consist of eight equal responds which continue above the capitals in the form of transverse and diagonal rib vaults. The transverse ribs above the aisles had to be heavily stilted because of the narrowness of the bays. The bases of the free-standing columns, which look exceptionally tall in our photograph, are in the two 15th-century western bays. The bridge-like reinforcing arches which span the aisles were not part of the original building but were probably added in the late 15th century.

An interior like this is not to be understood in terms of Umbrian or national Italian development. It is a remote offshoot of the French architecture of Poitou and Anjou. Admittedly San Fortunato was not the oldest Gothic hall church in Umbria to come under the French influence. San Andrea in Orvieto preceded Todi by some decades, even if that Gothic building remained unfinished after the wonderul start which had been made on it. Although the architect of San Fortunato may have been influenced by the form of San Francesco at Assisi where individual architectural features were concerned, he obviously had some personal knowledge of the south-west of France. This is clear from the gallery over the chapels, and the way he has lightened the walls and led the stresses inward. San Fortunato, the oldest and finest hall church in Umbria, established the form in the region: only twelve years later (1304) San Domenico, a hall church of much larger dimensions, was erected in Perugia (altered in the Baroque period); in the 15th century came the cathedrals of Perugia and Ascoli Piceno, as well as the Casa Santa at Loreto. But they are all far more Italian in feeling than their predecessor at Todi. There the delicate yet precise shapes of French Early Gothic can still be felt through the Italian bricks and mortar.

126 TODI   The Roman *nicchioni* (niches).
Formerly a two-storey substructure for a terrace dating from the Augustan period. The division between the two storeys is marked by a triglyph frieze with jutting moulding. It is not known what temple or secular public building stood above, on

the terrace. The beauty and tenderness of the design are typical of the Augustan period.

127, 128 TODI   Santa Maria della Consolazione. The church, begun in 1508, lies below the town in a meadow. The architect is unknown, for the Nicola da Caprarola (1508-12) who is mentioned at the beginning of its records can only have been the local foreman who carried out someone else's plans. During its construction, which lasted for a whole century, many important architects were consulted, among them Baldassare Peruzzi, Antonio da San Gallo the Younger and Vignola. The dome was completed in 1607.

It is no accident that this, the purest centrally-planned building of the High Renaissance, stands on Umbrian soil. The ideal of a regular building in the form of a Greek cross with a central dome – cherished by so many Renaissance designers, as plans and drawings of the period show – very seldom became reality, because it did not answer the needs of day-to-day church life. The Church decided to place the high altar in the centre of the space beneath the dome only in exceptional cases (for example, when a martyr's tomb was situated there). Thus the arm of the cross containing the high altar nearly always becomes larger and, of course, more important. At Todi the altar concha stands out because it has a semi-circular plan, while the other three arms terminate in polygons. It is significant of the difference between the Tuscan and Umbrian conception of space that in the most important High Renaissance central building in Tuscany, San Biagio in Montepulciano, quite near the south Tuscan-Umbrian border, the space under the dome is surrounded by four rectangles, while in Todi the same space is ringed by semicircular shapes forming a sort of gently-rounded clover-leaf pattern. In this church the style of the High Renaissance and the local Umbrian style blend together ideally.

If all the details of the building do not give the same harmonious impression, this is because it took such a long time to build and during this period architectural ideas changed. Thus the original plan never envisaged such a high drum, which owes its introduction to the Baroque passion for height. The interior arches at the crossing were probably intended to support a lower central dome immediately above them which would have united the four exedrae. The pilaster clusters which articulate the drum inside are far too powerful to belong to the period when the church was first built. The rhythmic alternation between broad window transoms and narrow wall surfaces on the drum has also resulted in the ribs which run from the base of the dome to the bottom of the lantern dividing the half dome into segments – an effect contrary to the Renaissance spirit. The features which date from the time when the building was nearing completion, for example the adornment of the arches at the crossing with rosettes and the exuberant decoration of the pendentive, are typically Baroque. Nor was it originally intended that the vaults of the shells should be pierced with windows at the bottom.

But these are minor blemishes which cannot really spoil the general effect. And since Bramante's ideas could not be put into practice at St Peter's in Rome, we have

163

the best example of the wonderful harmony which pervades every part of a centrally planned High Renaissance building in Santa Consolazione at Todi.

129 CARSULAE   The Arco di San Damiano. Because the Via Flaminia proper ran through Terni and Spoleto in post-Tiberian times, the branch of the road between Narni and Foligno was used only for local traffic and bits of the original Roman paving have been preserved in excellent condition. At Carsulae only one arch of the north gate through which the road passed remains. The town was destroyed by the Goths in the 6th century; in the fields on both sides of the Via Flaminia the remains of an amphitheatre, cisterns and other buildings can be seen.

107 Sheep-trough below Monte Vettore

109 Piano di Santa Scolastica

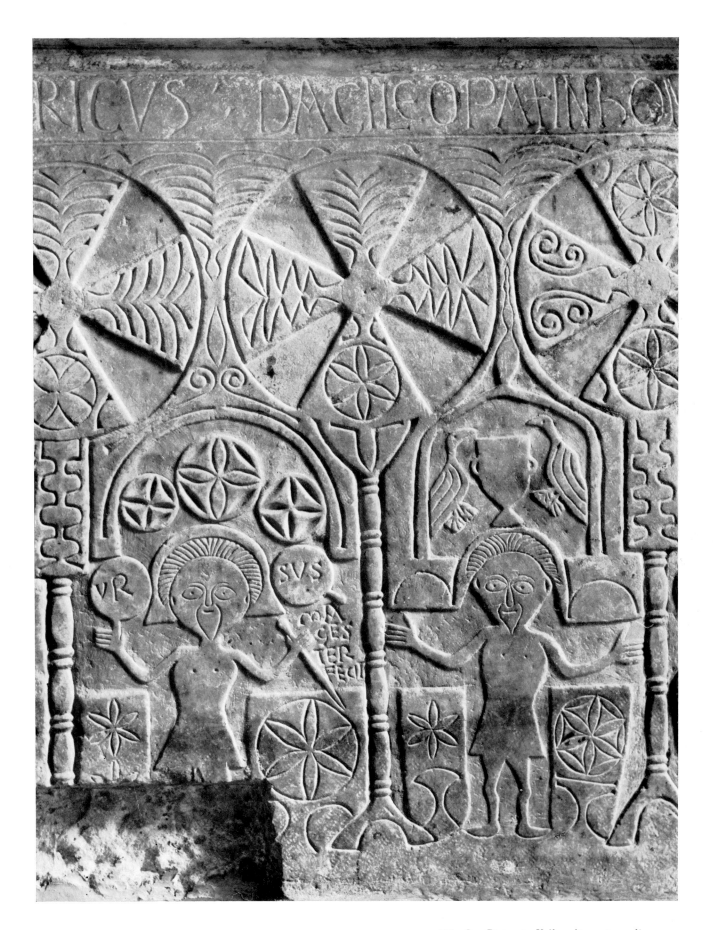

110   San Pietro in Valle: altar-antependium

111 San Pietro in Valle, near Ferentillo

112 Ferentillo, with the gorge of the Nera

113 Siesta in Ferentillo

114 Nitrogen works in the Nera valley, near Tern

115 The Cascata delle Marmore in the Nera valley

117   View of the Terni basin

118 The bridge of Augustus near Narni

121   Todi. The Cathedral

122   Todi. Piazza del Popolo, with the Palazzi Comunali

123   Ghirlandaio: The Crowning of the Virgin

124 Lo Spagna: The Crowning of the Virgin

125   Todi. San Fortunato

126 Todi. The Roman *nicchioni* (niches)

127—128 Todi. Santa Maria della Consolazione

130 ORVIETO from the south. The town lies on one of those tufa plateaux which are so characteristic of south Etruria and north Latium. The hill is 1,025 feet high at its highest point, 5,200 feet long and half as wide and falls away sharply on all sides. The Paglia and Chiana flow past its north-east side and join up south of the town to flow into the Tiber. This is, in fact, the plateau which extends furthest north, for 'the valley of the Paglia forms the natural boundary between the Etruscan highlands and the volcanic table land.' (H. Nissen).

Today Orvieto is situated very favourably from the point of view of communications, immediately above the railway and the motorway which connects northern Italy and Florence with Rome and the south. In 1958 the whole of Umbria exerted all its political, economic and cultural strength in a vain attempt to ensure that the *Autostrada del Sole*, planned to be the most important arterial road in the peninsula, should run through the centre of Umbria, roughly parallel to the Via Flaminia, and not via Orvieto. Two things emerged from this modern struggle for power over geographical communications: firstly that Orvieto was not a Roman town in the classical period and secondly that its position in modern Umbria owes nothing to any feeling of solidarity with the rest of the province.

In fact, as archaeological discoveries have proved, Orvieto must have been an extremely important Etruscan town, although its Etruscan name is still unknown. But it is equally certain that after this the plateau was uninhabited for centuries and that the earliest traces of Roman colonisation and culture did not appear before the 1st century AD. The present name only means 'the abandoning of a town', the exodus of a colony which could have taken place at any time. In 595 the Bishop of Orvieto signed himself '*episcopus civitatis Bulsinensis*', but a generation earlier Procopius of Caesarea, writing in Greek, had already called the town '*Ourbibentos*'. Finally it was called '*urbs vetus*' in the days of Pope Gregory the Great. Orvieto stands in an almost impregnable position to the north of the junction of the roads leading to Tuscany and Umbria; in classical times it was not even held to need a town wall and it must always have been one of the most important fortresses in Italy. East Goths and Byzantines encamped here on different occasions and Pope Alexander VI (a Borgia) and Clement VII, after the Sacco di Roma, also found a safe refuge here.

To the right of our photograph is the cathedral, to its left the church of San Francesco in which Pope Boniface VIII canonised King Louis IX of France in 1297. (The church was unfortunately given a Baroque restoration in the 18th century.) Roughly in the centre of the picture is the Torre del Moro (136 feet high), toward the left-hand edge the dodecagonal campanile of Sant' Andrea (12th century).

189

131, 132 The Abbey of SS. Severo e Martirio in the valley below ORVIETO. An ancient Benedictine foundation. When the monks came into conflict with the bishop's authority in 1221, they were banished and the abbey was handed over to the Premonstratensian order which had few establishments in Italy. The largest part of the building seems to be a development of a foundation by Countess Matilda of Tuscia in 1103, but it was restored and considerably enlarged after 1221 when the Franco-German order took it over. The idea of building a slightly-pointed barrel vault over a larger hall is a Burgundian one, but is derived from Cistercian ecclesiastical architecture, since even in the north the Premonstratensians had developed no architectural style of their own. It is surprising to find it in Italy. The wing of the monastery containing the abbot's house in the best preserved building of all, (plate 131), and sticks closely to Italo-Romanesque practice in its structure, resembling the Palazzo del Popolo in the town above quite as much as the Abbey of Casamari (south of Rome). In the Romanesque semi-circular arcades and the narrow notched friezes, reminiscent from a distance of a chess-board, there is no sign of northern French influences. The dodecagonal campanile dates from before the abbey was taken over by the Premonstratensians in the 12th century. Similar polygonal towers, used for defence, were familiar in Umbria in classical times. (See plate 68).

133 Etruscan necropolis near ORVIETO This necropolis, known as the *Crocifisso del Tufo*, consists of several straight roads with burial chambers thought to belong to the 4th century BC. The material used is giant blocks of tufa. The interiors of the graves are roofed in after various different fashions (with flat roofs, steep gable-roofs, etc.) but outside the graves are each covered with a single, low pyramid. The names of the corpses buried here are engraved over the lintels of some of the doors.

134 ORVIETO Palazzo del Popolo. Built about the middle of the 13th century of squared tufa blocks which have acquired a warm golden tone with the centuries. The palace's situation between two open squares meant that its ground floor had to be raised on open columned arcades, below which justice could be dispensed or markets held. One large hall occupied the whole of the upper storey, as in the town palaces of many north Italian towns (e.g. the Palazzo della Ragione at Padua or Vicenza). The building was extended in 1280 when the campanile was added. At the same time the ground floor arcades on the narrow western side were replaced by the present flight of steps. Much of it (for example the battlements, etc.) has been restored in the present century.

135 Etruscan vase (ORVIETO, Museo Faina).
This vase dating from the early 4th century is an imitation of an Attic vessel. On the neck is a picture of a fight between a gryphon and a stag, on the belly a conversation between two youths. Red-figure decoration on a black background.

136 ORVIETO The Pozzo di San Patricio. On the eastern tip of the plateau lies the *rocca* which the Spanish Cardinal Albornoz had erected here, as in many other Umbrian towns, from 1364 onwards. Close by but unconnected structurally is the great well which Pope Clement VII commissioned in 1528 when he fled here after the Sacco di Roma. He wanted to ensure that the town would be supplied with water in case of siege. Antonio da San Gallo the Younger designed the spiral staircase which winds round the outside of the central shaft of the well. To reach water it was found necessary to bore right through the upper layer of tufa; the well is 191 feet deep and 42 feet wide. All in all the staircase has 496 shallow steps, lit by 72 arched openings. The shaft of the well was first excavated out of the tufa; when the tufa ceased and the clayey tertiary layer was reached, the central framework was built of brick. It was completed in 1537, under the reign of Pope Paul III; hence the fact that the top of the well is decorated with his arms, the Farnese lilies. The medallion which Pope Clement VII had had struck, before his death in 1534, in honour of the well, bears the celebrated inscription '*Ut bibat populus*'. Spiral staircases were very popular at this period (for example, the Château de Chambord, Leonardo da Vinci's design for a *bordello*, etc.).

137 ORVIETO The Cathedral. The cathedral was built to commemorate the miracle of Bolsena, which resulted in the institution in 1264 of the feast of Corpus Christi, and to preserve and exhibit the Sacred relic. (The story of the miracle runs as follows. A Bohemian priest on his way to Rome was assailed by doubts about the miracle of transubstantiation. When he stopped to celebrate mass, however, his doubts were effectively answered, for blood issued from the Host.) In 1290 Pope Nicholas IV laid the foundation stone of this cathedral on the site of the previous Romanesque structure. The new building follows the pattern of the great mendicant order churches of the 13th century rather than the usual cathedral style.

138 ORVIETO View of the cathedral showing the left-hand portal of the West front and one of the two groups of five side chapels.

139 ORVIETO Façade of the cathedral. The façade, first added to the nave in 1310, is the latest in the line of 13th-century Tuscan cathedral façades (Siena from 1284 by Giovanni Pisano, Florence from 1294 by Arnolfo di Cambio). It resembles that of Siena Cathedral very closely but the emphasis on plastic effects which came naturally to the sculptor Giovanni Pisano is replaced by flat surface effects – again in a typically Umbrian manner. The mosaics at Orvieto, for instance, are allowed to play a far larger part than in Siena.
The actual builder of the church is unknown but the designer of the façade was Lorenzo Maitani who, though of Sienese origin, had become an Umbrian by adoption after working there for many years. His was the master mind behind all the different projects involved in construction: the actual building, the casting of large bronzes (the symbols of the four evangelists on the springing stones of the doorways and the

madonna group on the tympanum of the main doorway), the preparation and execution of the mosaics and the carving of the reliefs depicting biblical events which completely cover the buttresses between the doors, and the sides of the buildings up to the arches proper. No other 13th-century cathedral in the West could offer such vast surfaces for decoration with reliefs. This is yet another example of the Umbrian preference for a one-level surface. The charming way in which the front of the columns are criss-crossed by fine tendrils which curl up to form medallions (plate 140) or surround rectangular panels like garlands (plate 141) was probably adopted either from French stained glass windows or, even more likely, from French Gothic illuminated manuscripts. Recently it has been shown that 13th-century Byzantine embroidery exhibits exactly the same use of decoration for very similar iconographic subject matter.

After Lorenzo Maitani's death the work slowed down. In 1337 the arcaded gallery was finished, in 1354 the rose window was begun, while the tabernacle and the statues in the niches beside the window date from 1372. The row of apostles above the rose window was added under the supervision of Raffaele da Montelupo in 1560 at the earliest.

Whereas the sculptures and reliefs are original, the 14th-century mosaics have long since been spoilt by weathering and replaced by new compositions of later centuries, particularly the 17th and 18th. Between 1785 and 1789 some of the very oldest scenes were removed and sent to Rome as a present for Pope Pius IV.

140, 141 ORVIETO Carvings on the cathedral façade. In order to carry out such an extensive cycle of reliefs Maitani was forced to assemble sculptors of the most varying origins and abilities. The pupils of Giovanni Pisano cannot always conceal their north Tuscan training. The dramatic character of their art contrasts with the lyrical sensibility of the Umbrians. This is given its purest expression in the story of the Creation which takes up the whole of the northern, or left-hand, column. Never has the tragic story of our forefathers been related more gently and undramatically. Charm and innocence are dominating characteristics of these childlike faces even after they have sinned.

142 ORVIETO Interior of the cathedral. Its most surprising feature (as a cathedral church) is the absence of vaulting. This fact and the lack of any articulation of the walls (apart from encrustation) and finally the plain rectangular shape of the choir make the cathedral resemble the churches being erected all over central Italy by the Franciscans and Dominicans of that period. Apart from its actual dimensions the interior differs from that of a typical mendicant order church in two particulars. Firstly, it has three aisles. Whereas the majority of such churches have only a single nave which usually makes rather an austere impression, the gigantic round columns which separate the aisles in Orvieto strike a highly ceremonial note in the interior. Their wonderul capitals were fashioned by stone-masons of the school of Giovanni Pisano. Secondly, none of the mendicant order churches have chapels along the

outer walls of the side aisles as here (five on either side). Although they are rather close to each other they in no way break up the line of the outer wall of the nave, nor do they imply any visual extension of the interior or have the effect of blurring its outlines. The chapels remain remarkably isolated, passive and lacking in tension, in typically Umbrian fashion. The immobile calm interior with its absolute scale of measurements, open roof and inarticulated clerestorey has affinities with the Roman basilica of the Early Christian period.

143, 144 ORVIETO   The cathedral: frescoes in the Cappella Nuova by Signorelli. It is impossible to imagine a greater contrast than that between the two versions of the Last Judgment shown here, the one by Lorenzo Maitani on the façade and the other by Luca Signorelli inside the cathedral. And this difference is not due merely to the 200 years between them. It results from the strongly-marked individuality of two different artistic regions, the Umbrian and the Tuscan. To put it another way: the brilliant Signorelli could not and would not adapt himself to the Umbrian milieu. At first the commission to paint the chapel at the end of the southern transept went to Fra Angelico, who worked here from 1447 onwards with three associates, of whom only Bernardo Gozzoli is identifiable. But owing to Angelico's death and even more to the unfavourable political circumstances of the day, the work came to a halt when barely two of the eight panels were completed. One has to admire the artistic instinct of the patron who called in Fra Angelico and Gozzoli: no other Florentine artist could have assimilated the spirit of Umbrian art as well as they did. Signorelli (1499–1504), on the other hand, was completely uninfluenced by his Umbrian surroundings. Making no attempt to acquire the warm Umbrian palette, he used colours as bright and Tuscan and almost as cold as those of the mannerists. But these colours are applied so transparently that they only stress the drawing-in of the figures with single brush strokes and the cross-hatching which can be clearly seen.

The curve of the shoulder, the play of the wrists, the modelling of the thorax, are as accurate and precise as an anatomical drawing.

If the feeling behind the reliefs on Maitani's façade outside is predominantly lyrical, Signorelli's strength lies in his ability to portray the terrible. The artist is rather out of his element when characterising sacred and saintly personages; the expression on their faces is monotonously similar – Perugino was far better at this sort of thing. A wall niche to the right of the entrance to the chapel offered a natural frame for a single picture not connected with the general scheme of decorations. Primarily an intimate devotional picture for the individual worshipper, it is a *pietà* with the additional figures of St Faustinus and Pietro Parenzo, the first person to be buried in this chapel. He was a mayor of Orvieto who defended the town against heretics and was killed by the Patarenes in 1199. This *pietà* is more spiritual and reserved in feeling than the large frescoes.

145 ORVIETO   The western extremity of the town.
At the tip is San Agostino, in the background the Paglia valley.

130 Orvieto, from the south

131 The abbey of SS. Severo e Martirio: the abbot's house

132   The abbey of SS. Severo e Martirio, near Orvieto

133 Etruscan necropolis near Orvieto

134 Orvieto. Palazzo del Popolo

137   Orvieto. The Cathedral dominating the town

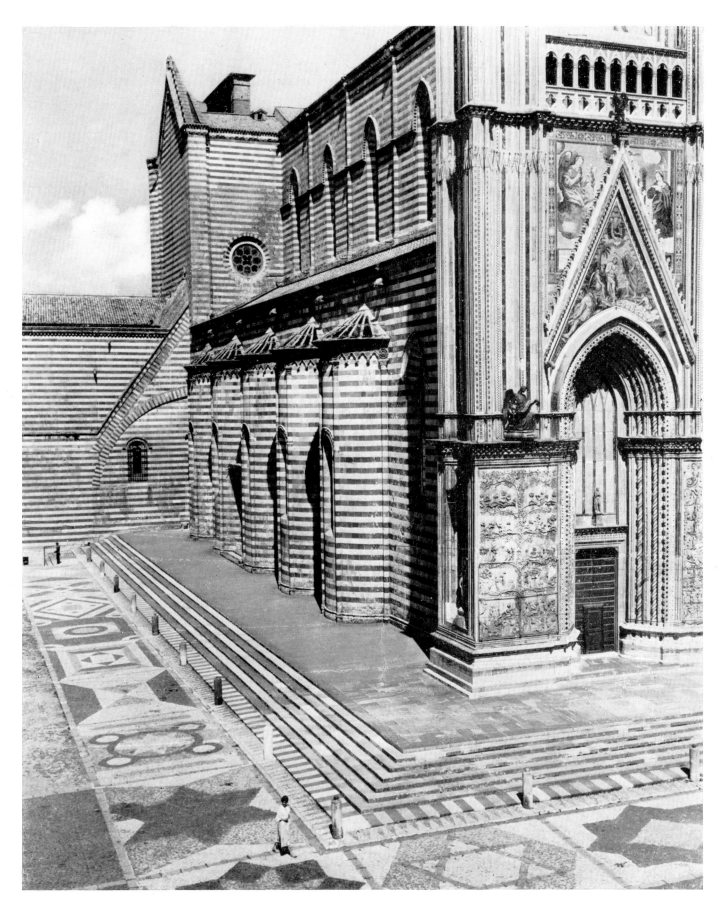

138 Orvieto. The Cathedral: side view

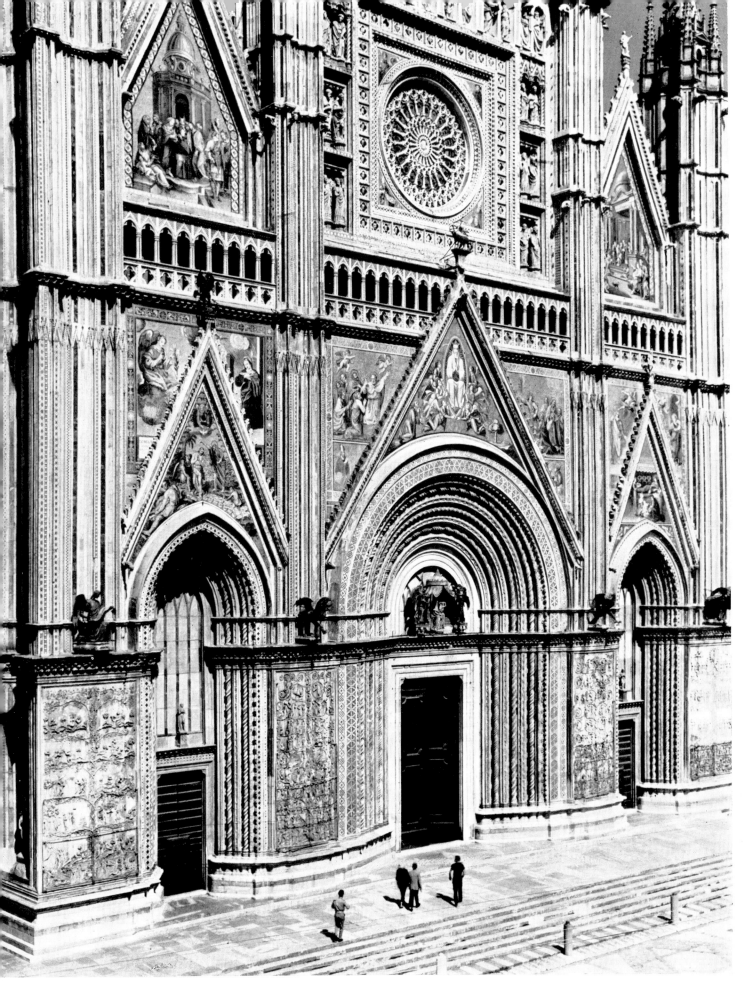

139   Orvieto. The Cathedral: façade

140 Orvieto. The Cathedral: detail of the façade

141 Orvieto. The Cathedral: detail of the façade

142 Orvieto. The Cathedral: interior

143   Orvieto. The Cathedral: fresco in the Cappella Nuova by Signorelli

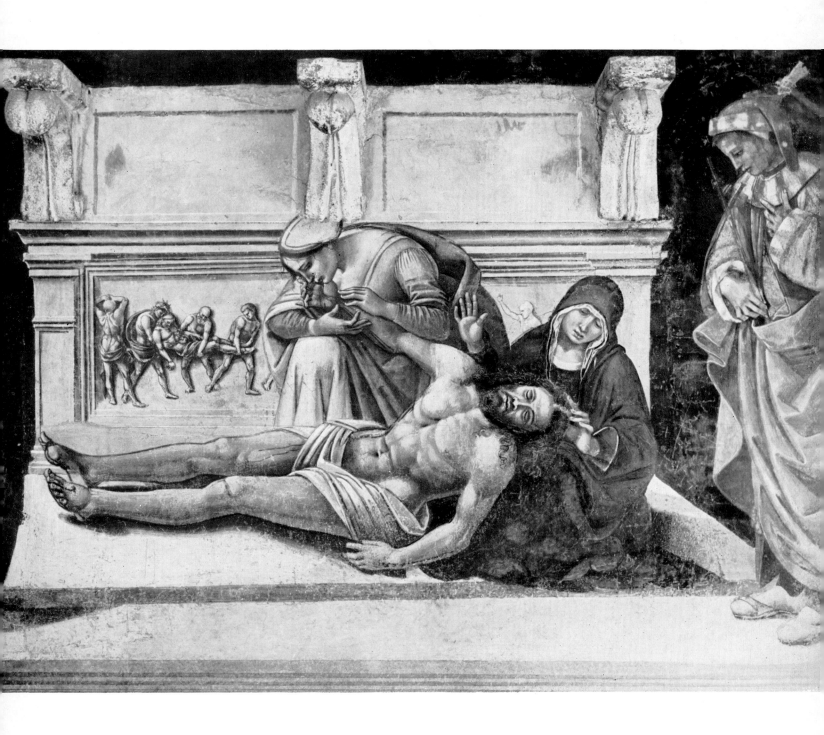

145 Orvieto. The western extremity of the town

BIBLIOGRAPHY

1 GEOGRAPHY

Umbria (Guida d'Italia del Touring Club Italiano), Milan, 1950.

BONASERA, F., DESPLANQUES, H., FONDI, M. and POETA, A., *La casa rurale nell' Umbria.* Florence, 1955.

MILONE, F., *L'Italia nell'economia delle sue regioni.* Turin, 1955.

RODOLICO, FR., *Le pietre delle Citta d'Italia.* Florence n.d., (1953).

WALKER, D. S., *A Geography of Italy.* London, 1958.

2 ARCHAEOLOGY

ASHBY, TH. and FELL, L., *The Via Flaminia, Journal of Roman Studies XI.* 1921, pp. 125ff.

BLOCH, RAYMOND, *Etruscan Art.* London, 1959.

GERKAN, A. VON and MESSERSCHMIDT, F., *Das Grab der Volumnier bei Perugia, Römische Mitteilungen 57,* 1942, pp. 122-235.

PALLOTINO, M. and HÜRLIMANN, M., *Art of the Etruscans.* London, 1955.

SHAW, CHANDLER, *Etruscan Perugia.* Baltimore, U.S.A., 1939. (John Hopkins University Studies in Archaeology, No. 28).

3 TOPOGRAPHY

CAMERON, M. L., *Umbria, past and present.* London, 1913.

HARRISON, A. M. and AUSTIN, R. S., *Some Umbrian Cities.* London, 1925.

HUTTON, E., *The Cities of Umbria.* London, 1925 (7th ed.).
        Assisi and Umbria revisited. London, 1953.

PATMORE, D., *Italian pageant: a tour through the cities of Tuscany and Umbria.* London, 1949.

RICCI, C., *Umbria Santa.* Translated by H. C. Stewart. London, 1927.

ROITER, F. and JAQUET, P., *Ombrie: Terre de Saint François avec un choix de Fioretti et le cantique des creatures.* Lausanne, n.d. (1955).

SYMONDS, M. and GORDON, L.D., *The Story of Perugia.* London, 1904.

4 ART AND ARCHITECTURE

BONELLI, R., *Il Duomo di Orvieto e l'architettura italiana del Duecento e Trecento.* Citta di Castello, 1952.

BORSOOK, EVE, *Mural Painters of Tuscany.* London, 1960.

CARLI, E., *Le Sculture del Duomo di Orvieto.* Bergamo, n.d. (1947)

CLARK, SIR KENNETH, *Piero della Francesca.* London, 1951.

GIOTTO, *Frescoes in the Upper Church, Assisi.* London, 1954.

GNUDI, C., *Giotto.* London, 1960.

JAMES, R., *Perugino: Umbrian School.* London, Medici Society, 1953.

KRÖNIG, W., 'Hallenkirchen in Mittelitalien'; *Kunstgeschichtliches Jahrbuch der Bibliotheca Hertziana,* II. 1938. p. 1ff.

MARLE, R. van, *The Development of the Italian Schools of Painting.* 19 vols. The Hague. 1923. Especially Vol. VIII, 1927 and Vol. XIV, 1933.

POPE-HENNESSY, J., *Italian Gothic Sculpture.* London, 1955.

ROTONDI, PASQUALE, *Il Palazzo Ducale di Urbino.* 2 vols. Urbino, 1950-51.

SALMI, M., *La Basilica di San Salvatore di Spoleto.* Florence, 1951.

TARCHI, U., *L'arte Cristiano-Romanica nell'Umbria e nella Sabina,* Milan, n.d. (1937). *L' arte mediaevale nell'Umbria e nella Sabina.* 2 vols. n.d. *L'arte del Rinascimento nell'Umbria e nella Sabina.* Milan, n.d. (1954).

UEBERWASSER, W., *Giotto Frescoes.* London, 1951.

VALSECCHI, M., *Piero della Francesca.* (Fontana Pocket Library of Great Art, no. 28).

WATSON, A., *The Imagery of the Tree of Jesse on the West front of Orvieto Cathedral (Fritz Saxl, 1890-1948, A Volume of Memorial Essays from his Friends in England),* London, 1957. pp. 149ff.

5 ST FRANCIS OF ASSISI

BOASE, T. S. R., *St Francis of Assisi.* London, 1936.

RAYMOND, E., *In the Steps of St Francis.* London, 1947.

INDEX

Figures in italics refer to plate numbers